Tammie has taken ~~[...]~~ and mixed it with biblical truth to make a true instrument of ministry. There are many people that still live in chains from past experiences with no knowledge or direction of how to break off those chains. This book is just another Moses that God has ordained to help lead many to the promised land of freedom.

—Darin Cochran, evangelist

Born out of many years of adverse relational distresses and agonizing personal issues, Tammie Hall has written a truly insightful and inspired guide for the many of us who may have been inadvertently subjected to emotional, psychological, and/or physical abuse. As a recovered and "now-blessed" former victim, she has thoughtfully and effectively connected these critical issues with time-tested scriptural truths and pertinent, divinely inspired solutions. May God bless each of you who both read and apply the principles contained in this wonderful book!"

—Del Delamont, multiple award-winning song-writer/composer, lifetime member of the American Society Of Composers, Authors, and Publishers (ASCAP)

Journey of Courage is a simplified, systematic approach in helping a victim cope with the effects of abuse. Tammie's personal experiences expertly lead the reader to a better understanding of themselves and their needs. Ultimately, the reader learns they are not alone, that Jesus loves them, and he cares.

—Bro. Larry Shuman, Sunday school teacher

Journey of Courage details a very unfortunate and troubled period of Tammie's life, and how she overcame this adversity through her deep faith in Jesus Christ, the Savior. In telling her story, Tammie will no doubt help the lives of hundreds of others that are suffering with major problems.

—Joe Trepke, Compass Building Systems, Inc.

Sister Yolanda Green,   Sept. 17, 2011

As you walk through this life, know
that if you walk with God, He will walk
with you.

Open your heart to His healing touch
and allow Him to bless you with an abundant
life filled with peace, joy, and love.

"Until we meet in Heaven, may the footsteps
along your journey of life always lead you
to God."

God Bless
you,
Tammie
Hall

Journey
of
Courage

Philippians 4:7

A healing workbook for those who've experienced
or are experiencing abuse

Journey of Courage
Tammie Hall

TATE PUBLISHING & Enterprises

Published by Tate Publishing & Enterprises, LLC
127 E. Trade Center Terrace | Mustang, Oklahoma 73064 USA
1.888.361.9473 | www.tatepublishing.com

Tate Publishing is committed to excellence in the publishing industry. The company reflects the philosophy established by the founders, based on Psalm 68:11,
"The Lord gave the word and great was the company of those who published it."

Book design copyright © 2010 by Tate Publishing, LLC. All rights reserved.
Cover design by Tyler Evans
Interior design by Lindsay B. Behrens

Published in the United States of America

ISBN: 978-1-61566-956-1
1. Religion / Christian Life / Women's Issues   2. Self-Help / Abuse
10.04.08

Dedication

With deepest love and gratitude, I dedicate this book to my Lord and Savior, Jesus Christ. Without his healing touch, I never would have had the strength to take my own journey of courage, much less share my testimony of healing with you. To God be all the glory for this book.

Acknowledgments

To my parents, Carl and Marie Hall, for their endless nights of worry, their love, and their prayers for me in spite of my issues before I allowed Christ to heal me.

To my beloved son, Jason, for loving me when he did not understand my ways and for leading me back to Christ. For his spiritual support, scriptural knowledge, his heart for Christ, and his love for his mother.

To my late husband, Ron. Before God called him home, he supported and encouraged me during the many late nights I spent working for the Lord.

To Marty, for his unconditional love and the friendship we share. Also for the many prayers he has prayed for me and his heart of service for the Lord.

To my childhood friend, Janet, for her ability to forgive me when I hurt her feelings, her willingness to help without question, and a heart of true friendship.

To the many brothers and sisters in Christ who prayed for me and helped me bring God's purpose for my life to fruition.

To my friends in healing for picking up this book and walking with me through the healing scriptures of God's Holy Word to find restoration of peace, renewal of hope, and a joyous life in Christ.

Table of Contents

"Be strong and of a good courage, fear not, nor be afraid of them: for the Lord thy God, he it is that doth go with thee; he will not fail thee, nor forsake thee" (Deuteronomy 31:6).

Foreword

I have known Tammie Hall and her family since she was a child. I lost track of the family during Tammie's teenage and young adult years, so I did not see her going through her years of anguish, depression, and healing. I do know her now as she walks with Christ as an exemplary Christian.

Tammie is my Sunday school teacher in a small Baptist church in Paulding County, Georgia. She is a lovely person who loves the Lord, and her "Jesus Light" shines ever so brightly. She is a great teacher, and her knowledge of the Bible is astounding.

She is truly anointed by Jesus Christ as you will see as you read her book. No one could have written this book without the anointing of the Holy Spirit. She admits she had reached the lowest point in her life before the tide changed and she found her peace.

Through *a Journey of Courage*, she shows us how to accept what happened and how to forgive. Forgiveness leads to God's ultimate peace, and her life was changed forever when she finally forgave her abuser. She takes us through the healing process and how to maintain the victory over Satan in our daily walk with Christ.

Pain and abuse is a part of life for a lot of people, but it does not have to destroy us. It can help us appreciate life in a fuller realization that if we had not gone through this trying time, we would not be the person we are today.

Please take the time to not only read but work through Tammie's book. I think everyone should. I never experienced anything of the magnitude that Tammie did, but I have had my share of battles in my life. After having read Tammie's book, I now feel better equipped to handle future trials that certainly await me. We cannot live for Christ without Satan constantly putting obstacles in our path. I feel that in addition to the Bible, I now have another weapon to fight Satan with—the instructions in this book.

—Frances Lindsey

Introduction

Abuse happens to someone every minute of each day. This painful reality—whether sexual, physical, or emotional—is a direct result of sin. However, those who have suffered at the hands of an abuser do not have to live a life of quiet desperation. Help is on the way, and his name is Jesus Christ. That is why I am bursting with joy that you decided to take your own personal journey of courage. The goal of your journey is to release the chains of bondage Satan has placed around your heart and find complete healing. This will be accomplished through the Scriptures in God's Holy Word. Through strength in Jesus Christ, you will shed the layers of pain and anguish from days past, reconstruct the present, and have renewed hope to live in continued peace and joy in the future.

This journey of healing is for those who have realized their life has not been exactly what they thought it would be. My personal abuse began with rape, but the ensuing years brought every abuse imaginable. Through the strength of Christ, I have overcome the horrible abuses of my past and now live in daily victory.

There are four steps you will need to secure before you begin your journey. I will remind you along the way, but it is ultimately up to you to follow through. Do not take these steps lightly, because they are very important.

Step 1: Create your personal *safe zone*. Pick a place that relaxes you and makes you feel comfortable and secure. Make sure when you are in your safe zone you will not be disturbed. Take the time you need for yourself to find God's healing on this journey.

Step 2: Always put on your armor of God and give him control over your thoughts. We will discuss this in detail in chapter two "Reflections."

Step 3: To aide in the healing process, you will be asked to participate in certain activities along the journey. I urge you not to skip over these sections but to respond and answer them truthfully. If you do not, you will be denying yourself complete healing.

Step 4: Cover yourself in prayer.

I am excited to get started on your journey, so get in your safe zone and let the healing begin.

Searching

I would like to personally welcome you to this incredible journey of healing brought to you through Jesus Christ. I also want to thank God for giving you the courage to pick up this book, and I pray that his mercy and love will abound as he opens your eyes and heart to the truth of his healing power.

It is imperative that you do not skip ahead or chose only certain portions of this workbook. Each chapter has been specifically designed by God to lead you through each stage of the healing process. You must completely accept Christ as your personal Lord and Savior in order to find what you are searching for. Therefore, if you are already a child of God, this journey will help you grow spiritually and find healing through Christ. If you have never asked God to be your personal Savior and you are willing to open your heart to Jesus and the healing that he has to offer, pray this prayer and believe it in your heart:

> Dear God, I know I am a sinner. I believe you were born of a virgin and died on the cross at a place called Calvary. I believe your blood paid for my sins. I believe you rose up on the third day and ascended into heaven. I pray now that you would forgive me of my sins of the flesh and make me whole. I believe in my heart and confess with my mouth that Jesus is Lord. Thank you, Father God, for forgiving me of my sins and sealing me with the Holy Spirit. I know I am forgiven and my name has been written in the Lamb's Book of Life. My salvation is complete in you. Thank you, God, for your saving grace. Amen.

If you prayed the above prayer, welcome to the family of Christ. The next step is to attend church and grow in Christ. You also need to tell a pastor or family member that has previously accepted Christ and arrange for baptism to make a public confession of your faith.

These two scriptures will encourage you to continue your journey:

> "Persecuted, but not forsaken; struck down, but not destroyed" (2 Corinthians 4:9).

"Knowing that the testing of your faith produces patience. But let patience have its perfect work, that you may be perfect and complete, lacking nothing" (James 1:3–4).

I would like to share a poem with you that I wrote during one of the more difficult seasons of my life. My walk with Christ was new, and Satan was trying to keep me in bondage. One day I was feeling very heavy and oppressed in my soul, so I sat down at my computer and began to question why I was feeling that way. I was a young Christian in my walk, not in life years, but I knew what I was feeling certainly was not of God. As I sat there in my depression, I began to ask God why I felt that way. I asked him what I was searching for. This poem is what God revealed to me about myself. These were the things that had been written on my heart during my years of abuse. I cried tears of joy after I finished the poem, as I knew God had spoken to me through it. It was a turning point in my healing process, and I thank God for loving me enough to gently show me the things he knew I needed to see in order to recognize the truth of *me*. I pray it will be a blessing to you also, but more importantly that it will help you recognize the truth of *you*.

"I've Been Searching"

I've been searching for a place called heaven.
I've been searching for a place called home.

I've been searching for a love so pure;
I've been searching, Jesus, for *you*.

I've been searching all of my life.
I've been searching to end this strife.

I've been searching for peace unknown.
I've been searching all alone.

I've been searching for forgiveness I know.
I've been searching to relieve this load.

I've been searching to lose these chains.
I've been searching to end my shame.

I've been searching for a healing touch.
I've been searching, feeling so much.

I've been searching to ease this pain.
I've been searching with nothing to gain.

I've been searching for a place called heaven.
I've been searching for a place called home.

I've been searching for a love so pure.
I've been searching, Jesus, for *you*.

I've been searching, Jesus, for *you!*

Have you been searching for the things this poem reveals? Have you been searching for peace, love, forgiveness, and healing? Have you been searching for Jesus? I know I was. I had accepted Christ, but I was still searching. This is where some of us get lost. We take the first steps in salvation and then we just get overwhelmed by Satan and feel defeated before we have read the last book in the Bible—Revelation. By the way, if you have not read it yet, once we accept Christ, *we win!* Satan is a defeated foe! Do you realize when we accept Christ he gives us authority over Satan? With authority like that, you should not be afraid to reveal what you have been searching for. Take the time to *reflect;* look within yourself and allow God to show you what you are searching for. You can write your own poem or simply share with God. He already knows what is inside of you; he just wants you to share it with *him.*

Dear God I'm searching for:

A pure heart, I'am searching for to truely to forgive myself when I make mistakes. I'am searching for when I lay awake at night to feel yur presence when I am praying, sleeping. I'am so searching for understanding.

Reflections

Now that you know what you are searching for, it is time to begin your spiritual journey of healing. Select an area that you feel most comfortable in, like your bedroom, sunroom, kitchen, or even your closet. Choose a place where distractions and background noises will not interfere with your personal quest. Turn off your cell phone. Get your pencil or pen and a diary, notebook, or paper, and, if you have one, your Bible. Create your *safe zone!* It is very important to be in your safe zone as you walk through this healing journey. However, remember that even though you are by yourself, you will never be alone because God will always be there with you. So get in your safe zone and let your healing begin.

Let us begin your journey with *reflection*. Reflection allows us to look back over the past events that have shaped our lives. God promises in his Holy Word to reveal the truth to us: *"And ye shall know the truth and the truth shall make you free*" (John 8:32). In order to see the secret truths we have stored in our heart, we must submit ourselves to Christ and give him authority over us. When we look in the mirror, all we see is our outward reflection, but God sees all of us, especially inside our hearts.

We give Jesus control over our mind to help us recognize the secret truths of our heart and understand how to make it pure again through Christ. Some areas of our heart are infested with Satan's trash. We have opened the door and let in anger, lies, and deceit. We have contemplated revenge with evil thoughts and thrown the best pity parties ever. Lust flirted with us, and we lay down in the bed of iniquity. Saying no simply was not an option!

Many of us have learned how to manage different areas of our life, but we seldom think about how to manage our thoughts. We must be like Jesus and deny any evil thoughts entrance to our innermost place: our heart. Thought management should be one of our greatest concerns. Without the ability to manage our thoughts, we cannot change our hearts. Proverbs 4:23 explains why we should be careful what we think: *"Keep thy heart with all diligence; for out of it are the issues of life."* Jesus desires for our hearts to be like his: fertile, fruitful, and full of peace, love, and joy. In simple terms, we must submit our thoughts to the authority of Jesus Christ in order to change our hearts to be like his.

Read the following statement and insert your name in the blank.

To have a pure heart, I ___yolanda green___ *must submit all of my thoughts to the authority of Jesus Christ.*

For us to submit our thoughts and prepare ourselves for battle, we must put on our armor and give God control of our lives every day. A few moments of prayer every morning prepares us for our daily battles. Ephesians 6:10–17 teaches us how to put on the armor of God.

1. Put on your helmet of salvation to protect your mind from Satan's lies.
2. Put on your breastplate of righteousness to protect your heart from evil darts.
3. Tighten your belt of truth so that you will have the courage to see and live God's truth.
4. Take up your shield of faith and hold tight to the sword of the spirit, which is the Holy Bible, because no evil can withstand the power of God's Holy Word.
5. Put on the shoes of the gospel so that you may walk in peace, sharing Jesus and the great things he has done in your life with the world.

6. Give God the authority to control your thoughts.

God's armor is the best way to protect yourself from Satan's lies. Every morning when you wake up, pray this prayer:

> Heavenly Father, I approach your throne in the name of Jesus Christ, and I stand in his authority as I come boldly before your throne with praise and thanksgiving, asking you to forgive me of my sins of the flesh (be specific and call your sins by name). I give you control of my thoughts today, and in complete faith I put on my helmet of salvation and breastplate of righteousness. Help me to tighten my belt of truth that I may see only your truth. Lord, help me to hide your Word in my heart, that it may be a lamp unto my feet and a light unto my path as I walk in the shoes of the gospel peace. Father, help me to pick up my sword of the spirit and my shield of faith so I can stand in victory with you. Thank you, Father God, for all that you do for me, and may your will always be done on earth as it is in heaven. In the name of Jesus, I pray. Amen.

I encourage you to create your own prayer, or you are welcome to use or revise mine. The most important thing to remember is to start each day by putting on your armor. God does not have a time frame for you to put it on, but the earlier the better. Lift your voice in song and put it on in the shower, or with a prayerful heart put it on in the car on the way to work; it is safer than calling someone on the cell phone. Anytime is a good time to be protected. Put on your armor of God every day and look forward to knowing God will be protecting you.

You should put your armor on now because you are going to reflect about the truth of your past and recognize how you coped with it. Pray the above prayer or your own prayer; then continue.

As children, teens, or even adults, when bad things happen to us, we often try to hide our faces and innermost feelings from those around us. We adopt the hear-no-evil, see-no-evil, speak-no-evil mentality. If we refuse to hear it, refuse to see it, and refuse to speak it, then we can *almost* convince ourselves it never really happened. At this point, we think we have successfully hidden the abuse in our secret place, our innermost being, our *heart.* The fact of the matter is that although we may think we have been successful in hiding it from the world, the truth still dwells deep in our hearts, and Jesus knows better than we do exactly what we have hidden there. "Can any hide himself in secret places that I shall not see him? Saith the LORD" (Jeremiah 23:24). God knows all of your secrets! The only person you are attempting to hide the abuse from is yourself. Often we go into denial and think if we ignore it long enough, it will go away. Unfortunately, it will not magically disappear but only take root and grow bitter weeds that choke out the positive elements of life. Satan's garden of evil is fertilized by deceit, watered by depression, and yields a crop of barren unhappiness.

The good news is, as we grow in Christ, he enables us to see the truth, and he also gives us the strength and courage we need to hear the lies, see the evil, and speak the truth. "The secret things belong unto the Lord our God, but those things which are revealed belong unto us" (Deuteronomy 29:29). God knows the truth, and he is the only one big enough to handle it. The beauty of God's love for us is that he does not expect us to handle it; instead, he is waiting for us to *give it to him.* "For nothing is secret that shall not be manifest; neither any thing hid that shall not be known and come abroad" (Luke 8:17). Nothing is secret to God, and all the things we have hidden in our hearts will be known and come to light. Satan's garden of evil does not thrive when the blessed light of Christ shines upon it. It is time for you to shed some spiritual light on the evil Satan has strategically planted in your heart, and start pulling up the weeds of unhappiness and bitterness.

This weeding will reveal the truth and nothing but the truth. These truths will be self-evident through the actions of your life—past, present, and future. Willingness to open the door of your heart and acknowledge the past, accept the present, and change the way you react in the future is the key to finding healing through Christ. "Lead me in thy truth, and teach me: for thou art the God of my salvation" (Psalm 25:5).

- You must acknowledge *what* happened to you *happened.*

- You must acknowledge *who* committed the evil act(s) of sin against you.

- You must acknowledge *when* it was committed and if it occurred only once or if there were repeated violations.

There may have been more than one person that sinned against you. You must acknowledge their acts of evil against you and recognize that it was *evil*, which is *sin* in its purest form. Through God's light you shall see the truth. This will help you understand what you did to survive and how you coped with the abuse.

"But this is a people robbed and spoiled; they are all of them snared in holes, and they are hid in prison houses: they are for prey, and none deliverith; for a spoil, and none says restore" (Isaiah 42:22). How often have you felt robbed and plundered? Are you snared in holes of misery? Are you hiding yourself in your personal prison house? This inner attitude allows Satan to constantly prey upon your heart and keep you in bondage. Satan's lies distort and destroy the good things Christ puts into your life. The ensuing self-destruction continues on a daily basis, resulting in anger and depression. God will reveal the holes in your heart, and he will fill these holes with fertile soil, plant new seeds, and grow the fruits of the spirit, in turn yielding a crop of happiness and joy.

Coping behaviors are linked directly to the abuse. Acting out comes from the secrets hidden inside the heart. If you have been trying to fill the holes in your heart with worldly things, this is your opportunity to ask God to help you identify them. Acknowledging the holes in your heart will weed out more of Satan's bitter roots. This weeding allows God to begin the restoration of your heart. Be honest with yourself, because God already knows what is hidden in the secret places of your heart. The following will help you identify your coping mechanisms.

Check all that apply to you:

- Anger—Short-tempered, quick to argue, or have a deep unspoken hatred

- Lies—Unable to speak the truth, living in constant denial of your past and/or present

- Pity—For others to feel sorry for you, loss of self-respect

- Addictions—Alcohol, drugs, gambling, pornography, sex

- Eating disorders—Anorexia, bulimia, gorging yourself with feel-good foods

- Self-Abuse—Cutting yourself, verbally beating yourself up, no self-love

- Revenge—Plotting evil acts against others, malicious behavior

- Obsessive Compulsive Behavior—Shopping, eating, sleeping, etc., which is demonstrating or "acting out" your feelings of worthlessness (lack of self-worth)

- Chat rooms—A place to hide from reality, live in a fake world with a fake identity

- Workaholic—No time for family, friends, church, no time to face the truth

Being successful in recognizing how your abuse affected your life is crucial to understanding your past and present behavior. Recognizing these behaviors does not excuse them; rather, it is a starting point for the healing process.

"And He shall be unto thee, a restorer of life and a nourisher of thine old age" (Ruth 4:14). Ruth's scripture tells us that he "shall be," not he might be or he could be, but he "shall be" our restorer of life. "And ye are complete in Him, which is the head of all principality and power" (Colossians 2:10). This is confirmation we can and will be complete in God, for he is the head of all principality and power. God even has rule over Satan! Thank God for his promise of restoration and completeness. He will be faithful to fill the holes in your heart with his fertile soil of mercy, love, and compassion. Open up to Christ and trust in him, because God creates each one of us with a perfect purpose in mind.

Satan knows that God has a plan and a purpose for your life. Through your abuser, Satan stole your joy and filled you with empty, aching holes. His goal is to keep you from completing God's purpose in your life. Acknowledging the truth of your coping behavior allows you to recognize the strongholds that Satan has used to bind you. Once you recognize Satan's strongholds, God's love will free you from them and restore you to the person he ultimately created you to be.

God loves you, and he can restore you by changing your:

- Anger into joy
- Lies into truth

- Pity into self-respect

- Addictions into self-control

- Eating disorders into health

- Self-abuse into self-love

- Revenge into forgiveness

- Obsessive Compulsive behavior into self-worth

- Chat rooms into church family and fellowship

- Workaholic attitude into time management

God is waiting for you to reach up, take his hand, and become the person he ultimately created you to be. He desires to restore you!

Do not allow the devil to hold you hostage anymore! Take God by the hand and do your battle. God has already declared victory, and his victory can be yours through a personal relationship with Christ. Weed out Satan's crop of barren unhappiness, and allow God to fill the holes in your heart with his holiness. Accepting the healing Christ has to offer will renew your life through repentance, deliverance, and restoration.

Allow God to begin this great restoration in you by answering the following questions that have been designed to help you see the truth of your past, identify where you are now, and learn how to give God your baggage. Do not be discouraged, because these questions are not designed to intentionally create pain; they are to help you in your healing process. *Do not dwell on the answers or get bogged down in the memories.* Briefly, yet truthfully, answer each question and move on to the next one. Before you begin, take these three simple yet effective steps in preparation for battle:

- Get in your safe zone.

- Put on your armor of God.

- Pray to God, asking him to reveal *his truth* to you through these questions and ask him to give you the strength, courage, and protection you need to answer them truthfully.

"Though I walk in the midst of trouble, thou wilt revive me: thou shalt stretch forth thine hand against mine enemies, and thy right hand shall save me" (Psalm 138:7). As you walk through your past, do not fear, for God is with you. Feel his hand upon you and his love within you. It is difficult to look back upon your life, but God understands the pain that is locked inside of your heart. He desires to set you free from Satan's chains of bondage. The things that will be revealed are truths, and "the truth shall set you free" (John 8:32).

To answer the following questions:

- Circle or check the appropriate answer(s) that applies to you

- Fill in the blank

- Write short sentences or paragraphs

Looking Back, Looking In, and Looking Up

(Questions for Truth and Healing)

1. Do you know for sure that you have been abused? _Yes_ or _No_

2. If you are not sure, what makes you think or feel that you have been abused?

   In past relationships
   and family member

3. How old were you when you were *first* abused? *I was* _23_ *years old*

4. Was your abuse a single incident, or did it happen repeatedly? *One time* *Repeatedly*

5. How many abusers have you had? I have had:
   One   Several   (Many)

6. How old were you when the *last* abuse occurred?
   I was 38 *years old*

7. Did you know your abuser? *(Yes* or *No*

8. Were they a family member, nonfamily member, or (both? *(Family)*   *(Nonfamily)*

9. If a family member, what relation were they to you?

   ___brother's___

10. If a non-family member, circle the answer that best describes your attacker:
    (Stranger)   *(Friend)*   *Kidnapper*   *(Rapist)*
    Co-worker   Peer   Casual Acquaintance

11. Circle the types of abuse(s) that were committed against you? *(Abandonment)* *(Emotional)*
    (Physical)   Psychological   (Sexual)   (Verbal)
    If sexual abuse was it: *Harassment   Oral (Rape)*
    Touching only

12. Did you tell anyone about the abuse? *(Yes)* or *No*
    If yes, who did you tell?

    _____

13. What was their reaction to your statement of truth about the abuse?

They told me that Jesus Christ will heal me, That I will be alright. That I am better now Jesus will make things ok with me

14. If you did not tell anyone, how did you personally deal with the abuse?

Very Emotionaly I felt I was alone in this world by myself, low self esteem

15. Do you feel you have dealt with your abuse and/or abuser(s)? *Yes* or (*No*) If no, why not?

Because I still reflect on it time to time.

16. Do you feel you are ready to find healing through Jesus Christ (*Yes*) or *No* If no, why not?

_____

_____

_____

_____

_____

17. Are you able to recognize and experience emotions? *Yes* or *No*

18. Circle the emotions you allow yourself to feel: *Happy* *Sad* *Angry* *Depressed* *Calm* *Lonely* *Confused* *Sexy* *Intimate* *Love* *Pain* *Anguish* *Joy* *Spiritual*

19. Do you allow yourself to cry? *Yes* or *No*

20. Check all that you experience: *Panic attacks* *Nightmares* *Uncontrollable bursts of rage*

21. Do you acknowledge your body when it feels hungry, pain, sleepy, or tired? *Yes* or *No*

22. Do you have a hard time loving and accepting your body? *Yes* or *No*

23. Do you have trouble expressing your feelings to others? *Yes* or *No*

24. Do you go numb or worry about going crazy? *Yes* or *No*

25. Do you abuse your body with alcohol, drugs, <u>food</u>, or sex? *Yes* or *No* If yes, which one(s)?

food sometimes

26. Does this self-abuse bring you gratification? *Yes or No* If *yes,* how long does the gratification last? _____ Is it worth it? *Yes or No*

27. Do you intentionally hurt yourself or cut your body? *Yes or No*

28. Do you have any physical illnesses as a result of the abuse? *Yes or No* If yes, have you consulted a physician? *Yes or No*

29. Do you have difficulty trusting people? *Yes or No*

30. Do you find it difficult to commit to relationships? *Yes or No*

31. Who are your closest friends?

_____

32. Are you in a healthy relationship now, or can you imagine yourself in one? *Yes or No* If no, why not?

_____

33. Are you subconsciously drawn to people that remind you of your abuser(s)? *Yes or No*

34. Do you cling to the people you care about? *Yes or No*

35. Do you repeatedly test people to prove their love for you in order to make you feel secure? *Yes* or *No*

36. Do you expect people to leave you? *Yes* or *No*

37. Are you able to let people love you? *Yes* or *No*

38. Do you find it difficult to actively participate in intercourse? *Yes* or *No*

39. Do you have sex because: *You are required to You desire to For other reasons* No

40. Do you enjoy the natural sexual desires God created you to feel? *Yes* or *No*

41. Do you feel sexual pleasure is bad or disgusting? *Yes* or *No*

42. Do you need to be in control during intercourse to feel safe? *Yes* or *No*

43. Do you use sex for favors, money, or to get what you want? *Yes* *No* *Not any more*

44. Do you understand the moral boundaries associated with sexual relationships? *Yes* or *No*

45. Do you have children? (If no, skip to question number fifty-one) *Yes or (No)*

46. Do you find it difficult to be close to your children? *Yes or No)*

47. Where your children are concerned, are you: *(Overprotective) Insensitive*

48. Is it difficult for you to set clear boundaries with your children? *Yes or (No)*

49. Have you talked with your children about sexual boundaries? *Yes or (No)*

50. Have you taught your children how to protect themselves against sexual predators? *(Yes) or No*

51. Are you close to your family or are you isolated and alone? *Close (Isolated and alone)*

52. Does your family know about your abuse? *Yes or (No)*

53. Does your family support you or have they rejected you because of the abuse? *(They support me) They reject me*

54. Do you expect your family to change? *(Yes) or No*

55. Have you accepted your relationship with your family? *Yes   or   No*

56. Do you or your family attend Sunday school and/or church?(*Yes*) *or   No*

57. If you do not attend Sunday school and/or church, when do you plan to start attending? *I plan to start attending Sunday school and church on:* _____

58. Does knowing you can find healing through Christ change your views about church?
(*Yes*) *or   No* knowing that he is real and he is my healer.

59. Are you mad at God? *Yes   or (No)*

60. Have you ever cried out to God for his help during or after the abuse? (*Yes*) *or   No*

61. Have you asked God to heal you since your abuse? *Yes   or (No)*

62. Do you believe in your heart Christ can restore your joy? (*Yes*) *or   No*

63. Have you prayed for forgiveness for any sins you committed during your times of distress? (*Yes*) *or   No*

64. Will you commit yourself to God's healing power? (*Yes*) *or   No*

65. Are you ready to exchange the way you live and think for worship and healing? Yes or No

66. Are you willing to forgive? Yes or No
    If no, why not?

_____

_____

_____

67. Are you ready to give yourself completely to God and find healing through the cleansing blood of Jesus Christ? Yes or No

Journal Exercise: No time limit. Write to God about the truth that has been revealed to you. Tell him where you have been, where you are now, and where you want to be at the end of this healing journey. (Use as much additional paper as is needed.)

Dear God, this is where I have been:

I've been in the world lhys ago. drinking and smoking blackmild, marijuana wanted to do what I wanted to do. I had been lost and abused misused, mistreated by friends, family members, verbally, physically, had felt no one love me, that I was all alone. I did'nt know who I was thow special I was.

Dear God, this is where I am now:

Now God where I am now is that I have you in my life. I knew life could have not been better with out you. I am free from the darkness of this world. In you have made my life complete I am not alone no more because I have you in my heart and in my life. I knew life could have not been knew better without you. Now I also knew that I am someone special in this world And that is I am the apple of your eye. That means a lot.

Dear God, this is where I want to be at the end of my healing journey:

LORD this is where I
wanted to be at the end
of my healing journey. Is
full of joy of you, that I
have and will win more souls
for the Kingdom of your bordling
laying hands on the sick to recovery,
strong and bless in my spirit.
Loving myself more and loving
others as well.

"I Know It's In There"

I know it's in there, but I don't want to see it.
I don't want to admit it. I don't want to share it.
Even though I reject it, I know it's in there!

I know it's in there, but I don't want to feel it.
I don't want to face it. I don't want to accept it.
Even though I deny it, I know it's in there!

I know it's in there, and I must see it.
I must admit it. I must share it.

I cannot reject it because I know it's in there!

I know it's in there, and I must feel it.
I must face it. I must accept it.

I cannot deny it because I know it's in there!

I know it's in there, so *I saw* it, and *I admitted* it,
and *I shared* it, and *I felt* it, and *I faced* it.

I know it's in there, so I *accepted* it!

The Choice

I pray God revealed the truth to you through the questionnaire. After all, you were searching for something when you selected this book, and you have taken the first steps to finding healing and restoration. Now it is time to understand how you became who you are.

In our searching, we often miss opportunities to better our life by making good decisions. A skewed perception leads us to make decisions that bring an unfortunate outcome. Once we understand how we are influenced by others, it is easier to make better decisions. Choices are set before us, and how we choose shapes our immediate and long-term future.

There are choices to be made every day of our life. No one is exempt. These choices shape our lives, and we live in the aftermath of past choices, deal with the uncertainty of present choices, and try to make better choices for our future. As humans, we are not always successful. What seems to be the right choice at the time of decision may turn out to be a disaster. The world seemingly offers a wide variety of choices, promising prosperity and fun, while a Christian lifestyle seems straight and narrow, wrought with peril. But the opposite actually applies. The lures of the world will eventually reveal their destructive nature, and when you fall from grace, no one will be there to pick you up. The world has a way of kicking you when you are down. On the other hand, God blesses his children daily. He will never leave us or forsake us. He is always there to pick us up when we fall. His ways are true and lovely. Knowing this, how can we willingly choose the wide road of the world when the narrow road has so much more to offer?

> "Enter ye in at the straight gate: for wide is the gate, and broad is the way, that leadeth to destruction, and many there be which go in thereat: Because strait is the gate, and narrow is the way, which leadeth unto life, and few there be that find it" (Matthew 7:13–14).

From personal experience, I can assure you the worldly gate is wide and the way is broad. I was searching for something I could not find, and absolutely nothing stopped me from self-destruction. Looking back over those years, it amazes me how many others were there in the world with me seeking their own self-destruction. The world could not give me the peace and healing that Christ has given me. I now realize the gate to everlasting life is straight and narrow, and truly there are few that find it. It is sad to think eternal life filled with peace is available to everyone but few accept it.

The more my heart becomes like Jesus, the narrower the world becomes, and I see the truth of events and circumstances in my life. It is beautiful to see life through the eyes and heart of Christ. As humans, we are not capable of handling life's problems, but Christ is, and when we give our burdens to him, there is great peace that comes to a weary soul. The past choices we made were influenced by the circumstances, events, and people in our lives *at that time,* and those choices have impacted and shaped our lives.

In order to learn how to begin making the right choices, we must first understand how our past choices were influenced by others. This understanding will help us make better choices today and for eternity.

How many times have you made a bad decision or choice and after the devastation passed you asked yourself, *Was that me?* You cannot believe you made such a bad choice. So you get busy beating yourself up, reliving how things might have been if you had only chosen differently. The question to be answered is, would your life have turned out the way your mind tells you it would have? Maybe it is Satan letting loose his mind monsters—set free to torment you and keep you in bondage, chained forever on memory row—replaying time and again the scenarios in your mind of how great it should have been if reality had yielded a completely different ending. There is no way we can know the future. Our human element renders us incapable of looking down the road of life and correctly choosing every good blessing God has intended for us. Only God is all knowing, and he alone is capable of choosing what is best for us. That is why we should allow him to make all of our decisions for us, big and small.

Our lives are often shaped by those around us, and it is quite amazing to realize the impact they have on us. Some are daily influences that take shape gradually and over time, while others are one-time impacts that immediately alter our entire way of thinking and reacting to real-life situations. Please understand that this does not excuse us from our behavior or release us from our moral and social responsibilities, but it does help us to understand how we made our decisions.

At this point, we cannot go back and undo our past decisions, but we can understand why we made some of our choices and change the way we make future choices. Here are several ways we were, and still are, influenced.

Was That Really My Decision?

If you have been, or are currently in a controlling or abusive relationship, then you should be able to identify a posture that typically represents a stance of authority, which immediately places a feeling of inferiority upon you, and any attempt to communicate with you is wrought with control. This allows the abusive person to take charge of the conversation and feed your brain with his or her voice inflection and tone to ensure that you perceive his or her meaning exactly the way they want you to. This type of posture and tone takes control of your brain filters and places what he or she wants you to hear in your brain. The result is *wrong thinking!* In turn, we make choices based on this wrong thinking and then wonder why we are so afraid to see the truth. Chances are, in a relationship like this, facing the truth would be confrontational, and it always seems easier for us to simply avoid the conflict by portraying submissive behavior. Nevertheless, the brain has stored this wrong thinking in its memory bank for Satan to use against you at an opportune time in the future.

Let's Make a Deal!

How often have you had to make a choice or decision and tried desperately to bargain your way out of it? Making another choice or decision is the last thing you want to do. It seems every decision you made before turned out to be a disaster, so why should this one be any different? At least that is what Satan wants you to believe. We try to deal our way out of having to make the choice or decision and eventually settle with what's behind the door of decision Satan picks for us. Of course, his choice is wrought with peril, as he has absolutely no intention of granting us one tiny speck of happiness. His sole purpose is to steal our joy and destroy us. He is the father of lies, and he is crouched like a roaring lion, waiting to devour us. His choice for us is guaranteed to be another disaster. By refusing to make an informed decision, we allow Satan to choose for us, and then we pay the price for it. Do not be afraid to make the right choice, even if it involves changes in your life or lifestyle. An informed decision is always better than Satan's deal!

Take a Chance!

Satan often places a pair of dice in your hands and tells you to go ahead and *roll*. He whispers in your ear things like, *What have you got to lose?* or, *Go ahead; I promise it will be fun,* and, *Take a chance; everybody else does it.* He encourages us to make the wrong choice! We know better than to do it, but we refuse to see the truth of the consequences of our actions. We lie to ourselves and think we will not get caught. We knowingly *chose* to take the wrong *chance* and then wonder why we cannot make good choices. Scripture tells us the devil is like a thief who comes only to steal our joy (John 10:10). Unlike Satan, God desires the very best for your life, and he is ready to record new beginnings with correct thinking and good choices—God's choices!

Conditioning!

As we grow up, we are conditioned and trained in our way of thinking. This conditioning comes from our home environment, educational and religious backgrounds, and social status. It does not matter if you are rich or poor or what the color of your skin is; the same sins apply to all lifestyles and races. The same abuses happen in every social status. No family is exempt from the dark forces that govern this earth! Even religiously devoted families have their battles with good and evil. *Everyone* is subject to Satan's lies regardless of his or her background. Often, it is difficult to separate people in our lives from Satan. However, to understand that people are not our enemy, we must realize Satan is the only driving force behind *every* sin. He manipulates people, institutions, businesses, and even churches into doing his dirty work for him.

Hiding behind them allows us not to see him with earthly eyes. All we can focus on are the *people* hurting us. It is even harder to see Satan at work in those who claim to be spiritual or godly people. But I can assure you: *no one* is exempt from the wiles of Satan, especially those who love the Lord. Knowing this, we should pray to God and ask him to give us spiritual eyes. God honors us when we truly want to see others through his eyes. Then we will see Satan *behind* the people, and the earthly principals associated with their vile behavior will be removed. God will grant us his love, peace, and grace. He will also restore our joy through his healing touch.

You should be able to see how you have been influenced in the choices you have made and realize how you can change these destructive patterns. There is only one obstacle that will continually stand in your way, and his name is Satan. You can not straddle the fence! It ultimately boils down to this: do you choose God who is good and offers peace and protection, or do you choose Satan, who is evil and offers confusion and chaos? Just something for you to think about the next time life requires you to make a choice or decision.

The Point Is

Whether you realize it or not, we make choices all of our life. A lot, or maybe most, of those choices are based on what others think and say we should do or our circumstances at the time. Understand you have a choice today not based on anything or anyone but yourself. Only you have the power to choose a better life for yourself based on the daily choices you make.

Choosing to follow Jesus Christ and daily walking in his ways by reading and applying his Holy Word to your life is the best decision you will ever make!

━━━━━━━━━━━━━━━

Thank you for allowing me to share what I have learned about our daily influences with you. I pray God will grow you and give you spiritual eyes to see and spiritual ears to hear. May you see exactly who your real enemy is and effectively recognize Satan's sneaky ways. It is up to you to personally make the choice not to give Satan another chance to choose destruction for you and your life.

Often we unknowingly enter Satan's playground through the choices we make, and he places us in bondage. However, we do not have to perpetually ride his carousel of chaos. In the next chapter, "Breaking Satan's Bondage," you will remove the chains that have been placed around you through cleansing prayer. But before you cleanse, you must take the time to reflect on the past and present influences in your life and see for the very first time how they have led you to where you are today. After you realize how you have been influenced, think about how you plan to remove the bad influences and replace them with godly ones. Share them with God in the space provided below.

Dear God, my past influences were:

_____

_____

_____

_____

_____

Dear God, my present influences are:

_____

_____

_____

_____

_____

Dear God, this is how I will make future choices:

_____

_____

_____

_____

_____

Breaking Satan's Bondage

Now that you have recognized how you have been influenced, it is time to begin your journey along the narrow pathway. Take God's hand, and he will lead you to the healing that he has waiting for you. You have chosen wisely, as this is a great turning point in your life. So head for the narrow road and see what God has in store for you!

Following is a prayer that has been designed to break the chains of Satan's bondage, as well as the curses that have been placed upon your life. Often, we unknowingly open the portals of hell and invite these curses into our lives. Some curses are handed down from generation to generation, and unless they are removed, they will continue to be handed down to future generations. The Bible acknowledges generational sins; therefore, we should also acknowledge them. "Then answered all the people, and said, his blood be on us, and on our children" (Matthew 27:25).

Read through the prayer first and insert what applies to you individually where requested. Stay sensitive to anything the Holy Spirit reveals to you and write it down in the space that has been provided. Once you have completed filling in the prayer, start at the beginning and pray it all the way through without interruption from beginning to end and mean it in your heart.

Before you begin praying this prayer, get in your *safe zone*, as this is an exclusive meeting between you and God. Pray this prayer out loud and speak openly and audibly to God.

Breaking Satan's Bondage Prayer

Dear Heavenly Father:

I come before you in the name of your precious Son and my Savior, Jesus Christ. I humbly yet boldly enter your gates with thanksgiving and come into your throne room with praise. I am overwhelmed by your gracious mercy and love for me, and I thank you in advance for the forgiveness of my sins and the positive spiritual changes that you are bringing to my life.

Lord, I come before you now in agreement and to make a covenant with you because you alone are God and you rule over all of heaven and earth. Because you are the one true God, you keep your covenants of love, forgiveness, and mercy with those who love you with a pure heart and obey your commandments. I pray now that your ears will hear and your eyes will see the heart of this prayer from your servant. I humbly bow before you and confess my present and past sins and the sins of my forefathers and every transgression we have committed against you. Please show mercy and forgiveness, Lord, for we have sinned mightily against you. I ask now that you remove the shame that I have been covered with because of the evil acts of sin that were committed. I ask you to cleanse my heart and take away the sin and shame that has kept me bound along the journey of my life until now.

Supernatural Bondage

I ask forgiveness for and rebuke my sin and the sins of my forefathers for any and all involvement in witchcraft, occults, or participation in the supernatural realm. From this moment forward and for all eternity, release us from Satan's bondage and forgive us, Father God, for the following participation in witchcraft, occults, or the supernatural realm, including astrology, séances, horror movies, wicked games, demonic books, casting of spells, fortune telling, and any other participation that caused us to sin against you. Father God, I ask forgiveness for and I renounce my involvement and participation in these wicked sins, and I break their curse off my life and off the lives of my children, their children, and their children's children.

Father God, forgive me for these supernatural sins:

_____

_____

_____

_____

_____

Addictive Bondage

I ask forgiveness for and rebuke my sin and the sins of my forefathers for any and all involvement with drugs, alcohol, or any addictive substance. From this moment forward and for all eternity, release us from Satan's bondage and forgive us, Father God, for the following participation with drugs and alcohol abuse. Father God, I ask you now to close any doors our involvement opened in the spirit realm related to the sins of addictive bondage, depression, and oppression.

I specifically renounce my involvement with the following drugs, including tobacco use, and I break the power of their curse off my life and the lives of my children, their children, and their children's children:

Sexual Bondage

I ask forgiveness for and rebuke my sin and the sins of my forefathers for any and all involvement in sexual sin. I ask you, Father God, to remove all impurity, perversion, incest, and promiscuity from me and my children, their children, and their children's children from this moment forward and for all eternity. I ask that you release us from all of Satan's sexual bondage, which may include rape, molestation, harassment, touching, oral, pornography, and any sexual behavior that pertains to or permits sexual impurity, perversion, incest, and promiscuity.

Father, I renounce the hold of every perverted and promiscuous image that Satan has bound me with. Forgive me for allowing unclean and perverted images before my eyes. I will stand upon Psalm 101:3: "I will set no wicked thing before mine eyes: I hate the work of them that turn aside; it shall not cleave to me." I will not willingly allow any vile thing to come before my eyes now and in the future. Father, I ask you now to take the sword of your spirit and sever every ungodly sexual tie between me and the people that I knowingly had sexual behavior with, whether male, female, or multiple partners.

Father, I also ask you now to take the sword of your spirit and sever every ungodly sexual tie between me and the people that have violated me sexually without my consent whether I know their names or not. Father God, I pray now that you would forgive me for any and all mental lust and emotional relationships that I participated in without intercourse that should have been reserved for my husband or wife.

Father, I am asking you to release your angels to retrieve the fragments of my soul from these men and/or women. Restore them to me by your Holy Spirit so that I might become spiritually whole, free of sexual bondage, and set apart for you and your guidance. I rebuke every unclean spirit and ask you to release it and its influences from my life. Father God, please forgive me for the following unholy sexual behavior(s) with the known people listed below and/or those that you know committed acts of sexual sin against me, and release me from the unholy sexual bondage that Satan bound me with whether the sexual acts were willful or forced:

_____

_____

_____

_____

_____

Thank you, Lord, for washing me in the cleansing blood of your son and my Savior, Jesus Christ, for his blood alone has the power to cleanse and atone. I dedicate my mind and body now as your temple; by the power of your Holy Spirit, remove all defilement of the spirit, soul, and flesh from this earthly sanctuary. Fill me to overflowing with the indwelling of your Holy Spirit. Open my eyes so that I may see spiritually. Open my ears so that I may hear spiritually. Prepare my heart to receive all that you have in store for me. *I am yours,* Lord. Have your will and your way in my life from this moment forward. Amen.

What a prayer! You should have felt the weight lifting off of you with every renouncement of sin, and Satan's chains of bondage should have fallen out from around you! God truly is an awesome God. It is very important to keep your covenant with God. He is making good on his promise for healing, as he has already shown you how to break the chains of your past and present bondage and prevent future bondage from your children and grandchildren.

The next stage of the healing process is recovery. In order to recover from our abuse, we must erase our worldly and victim viewpoints from our hearts and replace them with instructional scriptures found exclusively in God's Holy Word. In the next chapter, we will take a scriptural stroll down "The Road to Recovery" and begin writing God's scriptures in our hearts.

The Road to Recovery

Now that you have been spiritually cleansed through prayer, do not allow Satan to make you feel like you have to go through difficult times alone. With God we are never alone! He tells us in his Holy Word, and he proves it to us time and again as we journey through life with him. It is easier to trust someone who always keeps his word, and I can assure you that God always keeps his word. I hope you are excited to find out what else he has in store for you as you continue your personal journey of healing.

Speaking of healing, a scriptural road to recovery lies ahead. This road is filled with instructional words from God, which, if followed, will teach you how to begin changing your worldly views and your heart. He left his Scriptures here for us to read so that we might learn and grow spiritually. Read the following scriptures to find out how God's Holy Word will help you continue recovering from your past, change your present, and prepare you for your future.

―――――――――

Trust God―"Trust in the Lord with all thine heart; and lean not unto thine own understanding: In all thy ways acknowledge him and he shall direct thy paths" (Proverbs 3:5–6).

Proverbs instructs us to trust God with all our heart in everything we do, even if we do not understand it at the time. God has only the best in store for us. That is why you should allow him to direct your path throughout your life. He sees the big picture, while we only see one snippet at a time.

―――――――――

Hide God's word in your heart―"Thy word have I hid in mine heart, that I might not sin against thee" (Psalm 119:11).

If we hide the Word of God in our hearts, we will not be as likely to sin against him. We may read God's Word, but if we do not attempt to memorize it or write it in our hearts, then we fall short when it comes to living it. The Holy Bible is our sword and shield, and it is a vital defense against Satan. Remember, it is part of God's armor.

―――――――――

Love and serve God with all your heart and all your soul—"I command you this day, to love the LORD your God, and to serve Him with all your heart and, with all your soul" (Deuteronomy 11:13).

The first commandment is to love and serve God with all your heart and soul. This commandment prepares the way for us to love ourselves and others, even those who are evil and wicked. We are called to love the sinner but not the sin! We are also called, as God's children, to pray for the wicked.

———————

Love your neighbor and love yourself—"Thou shalt love the Lord thy God with all thy heart, and with all thy soul, and with all thy strength, and with all thy mind; and thy neighbor as thyself" (Luke 10:27).

The first thing we must do is love the Lord our God with everything within us, including our strength and our minds, "and thy neighbor as thyself." It is very difficult to love someone else if you are unable to love yourself. Furthermore, you cannot love yourself until you love God. We often forget that God is love, and without truly understanding how we are supposed to love God, it is hard to understand how to love ourselves, much less anyone else, including our neighbors! In order to heal, you must start loving God, yourself, and your neighbor. For without love, there is no God, and without God there is no hope!

Find your strength in the Lord and do not be afraid—"The Lord is my light and my salvation; Whom shall I fear? The Lord is the strength of my life; of whom shall I be afraid?" (Psalm 27:1).

The Lord is our light and our salvation. He is also our strength! When we stand with God, we do not have to fear or be afraid of anyone. God has given us his protection. His Holy Word is our protection! That is why we must hide it in our hearts. Remember, Satan is our only real enemy, and God told us in Ephesians 6:10 how to put on our armor of God and how to fight Satan with the sword of the spirit and the shield of faith, which is God's Holy Word! So whom shall we be afraid of or fear! All evil acts are manipulated by Satan, and God tells us to "submit yourselves therefore to God. Resist the devil, and he will flee from you" (James 4:7). We stand victorious in Christ as we draw our strength from him. Jesus, through these few scriptures, has shown us how to love him, ourselves, and others by changing our hearts. The challenge for you is to follow God's Holy Word and live it daily.

Walk as a child of God and let the light of the Lord shine in you—"For ye were sometimes darkness, but now ye are light in the Lord: walk as children of light" (Ephesians 5:8).

We were once in darkness, but now we are in the light of the Lord. God has brought you out of the dark by releasing you from Satan's chains of bondage and forgiving you of your sins. It is time for you to let the light of the Lord shine through you for others to see. There is no more room for darkness in your heart. Bask in the glory of the light of the Lord and see things in a whole new spiritual light.

Enjoy the peace of God—"And the peace of God which passeth all understanding, shall keep your hearts and minds through Christ Jesus" (Philippians 4:7).

Now this is profound! The "peace of God" will keep our hearts and minds "through Christ Jesus." Have you ever met someone and you sensed something special about him or her? He or she seemed to have a glow, and no matter what the situation, he or she was always calm, never becoming rude or worried, just exuding an element of peace. He or she was always willing and ready to help, to pray, or to serve, and he or she always had words of encouragement. You could tell by his or her actions he or she loved the Lord, him or herself, and everyone around him or her. He or she had a peace through Christ Jesus that surpassed all understanding. I have known people like that, and when you truly walk with Christ in your heart, evil is blinded by the light. If we change our hearts to be like Jesus, then we too can glow with the light of the Lord, exude an element of peace, and blind evil. There is no peace like God's peace!

———————————

Let God guide the paths of your life and find the fullness of his joy—"Thou wilt shew me the path of life; in thy presence is fullness of joy; at thy right hand there are pleasures for evermore" (Psalm 16:11).

This psalm is music to my battle weary ears! It also encourages us to let these scriptures awaken our hearts. This healing road to recovery has shown us that God will show us the paths of our life. If we want the fullness of joy that comes from being in the presence of the Lord and we desire his "pleasures for evermore," then we must daily apply what we have learned on this scriptural road to our lives. God is laying a firm foundation, and every stone of healing must be put in place.

The Point Is

The road to recovery begins with changes in our heart. Through prayer and following God's Word, we are able to shed spiritual light on Satan's lies and deceit, in turn breaking more chains of bondage. We cannot see through the eyes of Christ or feel with his heart if we hold onto our dark secrets. As children of light, we must continue to release the bondage from our hearts by changing the way we perceive things, how we think about things, and how we react to situations. This can be accomplished by applying the teachings in the Scriptures. The Bible is our instruction manual for a peaceful life. All we have to do is read it, believe it, and apply it.

In struggling with our pain, we perceive things from a worldly, victim viewpoint. We think things that are not pure or holy, and we react in the flesh. These victim viewpoints lose their powerful strongholds when we see things from a spiritual perspective, allowing us to feel and react differently to the same situation or new ones that arise daily. Remember, Satan sets no boundaries, and nothing is sacred to him.

By putting on our armor and giving God control of our thoughts daily, we are able to stand firm against the spiritual battles that rage around us. We must not allow the devices of the devil to defeat us. As God's children, we are already victorious! We will face opposition when we rebuild our lives for God's purpose. Satan will try to keep us in bondage, as he strongly opposes the reconstruction of our hearts. When we apply God's Holy Word to our heart, the light of Christ shines in the darkest corners where Satan dwells, and he has no choice but to retreat from the blessed light.

But be assured; he will be back like a thief in the night to try and steal your joy, disrupt your peace, and dash your hopes with his lies and deceit, so stay prepared for the battle daily!

At this time, take a moment to reflect about what should be written in your heart and how you are supposed to love. Share with God the changes you are going to personally make to better your life one scripture at a time.

Dear God, this is how I will apply these scriptures to my heart so that I may enjoy your peace and fullness of joy in my personal life:

I want to have the LORD AND my Enemies as thy self Luke 10:27 Also stay postive and view things in a better Respetive way Phill 4:9 to always trust In you God when I face obstacles and difcult things in my life. Proverbs 3:5, 6

Introducing Satan

I hope you were able to write the scriptures God shared with us on "The Road to Recovery" upon your heart. It is necessary to realize that Satan is the only real enemy we have and to understand his evil mission is to keep us bound. God's scriptures prepare us for the daily battle we face between good and evil. There is a lot more for us to learn as we grow in our Christian walk, and when we walk with God, the world looks different. To help us understand our adversary better, it is time to boldly go forth in the name of the Lord and learn more about whom Satan is and his nasty battle tactics.

The Bible tells us everything we need to know about Satan. He is Lucifer, the fallen angel of light, "for Satan himself is transformed into an angel of light" (2 Corinthians 11:14). "How art thou fallen from heaven, O Lucifer, son of the morning! How art thou cut down to the ground" (Isaiah 14:12). We know him as Beelzebub: "But some of them said, He casteth out devils through Beelzebub the chief of the devils" (Luke 11:15). The devil takes the form of a dragon and a serpent or snake, and this great deceiver is also named Satan. "And the great dragon was cast out, that old serpent, called the Devil, and Satan, which deceiveth the whole world: he was cast out into the earth, and his angels were cast out with him" (Revelation 12:9).

It is imperative for us to understand that Satan is our only adversary. He comes to steal our joy, kill our peace, and destroy our faith! "The thief cometh not, but for to steal, and to kill, and to destroy" (John 10:10). He sends his wicked angels disguised as false prophets to deceive us: "Beware of false prophets, which come to you in sheep's clothing, but inwardly they are ravening wolves" (Matthew 7:15). We must write the scriptures upon our hearts in order to know the difference between God's truth and Satan's lies. First Peter 5:8 instructs us to "be sober, be vigilant; because your adversary the devil, as a roaring lion, walketh about, seeking whom he may devour." Satan has a counterfeit for every good thing that God gives us, and he constantly seeks to devour us.

When we begin to see Satan through spiritual eyes, we are able to discern the true differences between good and evil. We are equipped to recognize Satan's manipulations as he uses people around us to perform his wicked deeds and evil acts. In this battle between good and evil, we become walking, talking targets every moment of every day. Satan comes to steal the light of God, our Jesus light! If he can steal our joy, then ultimately he will be able to destroy our way of thinking and kill any hope of peace we have. Satan can subtly deceive us through things that look good, at least at the time of his deception. Then when he has us in his snare, he dumps all his evil on us and drowns us in darkness and depression. We cannot see him because our spiritual eyes have been blinded, and our spiritual ears have been deafened. At this point, he wants us to believe that he has power over us, and he does until we call on Jesus! Then the blessed light of Christ enters the darkness and drives Satan away, and we are able to see the truth once again.

Incredibly, we have come full circle from where we started in the beginning about recognizing the truth—the truth of how Satan has used, and perhaps still uses, people in our lives to influence and change us. God's Holy Word teaches us about Satan, and these scriptures are powerful because they are God's knowledge, which is the key to recognizing and defeating Satan.

God's healing process has other steps that are just as important as understanding Satan. This knowledge will keep you steadfast on your journey and help you recognize when Satan is trying to undermine you. Because Satan orchestrates battles of spiritual warfare, it is extremely important to put on your armor of God and hide his Holy Word in your heart daily.

The Point Is

The devil will try to destroy the healing process with his lies. Remember, the devil is the father of all lies. He has no good intentions for your life, and he desperately wants to prevent you from reclaiming your joy and peace. He comes only to steal, kill, and destroy! Satan roams the earth to and fro, seeking whom he may devour. No one is exempt from his fiery darts of deception. He will try to devour you through various oppositions. He uses anyone he can to further his wickedness. He is relentless and will come at you until he finds no cracks left in your armor to seep through. He is your only adversary; that is why you must learn his ways. God's Holy Word describes Satan and his tactics so we may recognize them and thwart or deflect his wicked darts. We must prepare ourselves for battle daily by putting on our armor of God, give him control of our thoughts, and hide the Scriptures in our hearts.

Satan must flee at the name of Jesus and retreat when the Holy Word of God scalds him. The light of Christ illuminates the dark recesses of the wicked one's cellar and withers the roots of deception. With Satan, no one and nothing is sacred. We all are his targets and have been since his fall from heaven and

God's glorious grace. We will remain as such until the Lord comes to call his children home, binds Satan and casts him into the pit of hell for eternity. Only then will we be completely free of Satan and his treacherous ways.

Take few moments to ponder the things God has taught you about Satan and his wicked ways. Apply this new and powerful knowledge of how Satan works to a difficult experience or experiences in your past and apply it to a current situation you may be in. Share your thoughts with God.

Dear God, this is what you taught me about Satan and his battle tactics through your Holy scriptures:

2 corinthews 10:4

Dear God, this is how Satan has deceived me in the past and used his wickedness against me:

persude me with words

_____

_____

_____

Dear God, this is how Satan is trying to deceive me and how he is using his wickedness against me now:

_____

_____

_____

_____

Battles Above Us

Once we understand more about Satan and his wicked ways, we are less likely to fall victim to his treachery. However, it is extremely important for us to remember that battle skirmishes happen daily. In fact, there are battles raging just above us right now! These battles are between God's warrior angels and Satan's warrior angels. Yes, even Satan has angels, however wicked!

These battles above us in the realm of the heavenlies are spiritual warfare. Spiritual warfare is a conflict between the spirit and the strongholds of the flesh. These battles are fought on our behalf before they ever reach earth! God loves us so much that he has his angelic warriors intercede and often intercept our battles; in other words, they fight Satan for us to help keep us pure and holy.

We know that spiritual warfare happens because the Bible tells us so.

For though we walk in the flesh, we do not war after the flesh. For the weapons of our warfare are not carnal, but mighty through God to the pulling down of strong holds. Casting down imaginations, and every high thing that exhalteth itself against the knowledge of God, and bringing into captivity every thought to the obedience of Christ.

2 Corinthians 10:4

The scripture states that "we walk in the flesh" but the "weapons of our warfare are not carnal," which means flesh. Instead, the weapons we use are "mighty through God." Our weapons are the armor of God, the Scriptures, which are our sword and shield, and prayer and obedience toward God. Our godly and spiritual weapons pull down the "strongholds" Satan has over us, which helps us when it comes to "casting down imaginations," meaning arguments, and brings us into our obedience with Christ. In simple language, God's angels fight Satan's angels for us, but we must also do our part in pulling down the strongholds. How marvelous it is to know that God has his greatest warriors battling on our behalf, helping to safeguard us from Satan's snares.

Because there will always be conflict between the spirit and the strongholds of the flesh, we must not allow ourselves to succumb to sinful temptations, lest we surrender ourselves to Satan's bondage. However, if we walk in the Holy Spirit, we will be better prepared for spiritual warfare. We will begin to recognize sinful temptations and turn from them. We will be able to maintain our freedom through Christ.

Galatians 5:16–18 teaches us to walk in the Holy Spirit in order to avoid fulfilling the temptations of the flesh. "This I say then, walk in the spirit, and ye shall not fulfill the lust of the flesh. For the flesh lusteth against the spirit, and the spirit against the flesh: and these are contrary the one to the other." When we allow the Holy Sprit to lead our lives, we are not bound by the lusty law of Satan's world. Unfortunately, because we are made of flesh, we are not always successful in continually walking in the Spirit. Of course, only God's children are able to walk in the Holy Spirit; therefore, those who reject God are always bound by Satan and his wicked ways.

Satan's ways are certainly not God's ways, so the world is full of the works of the flesh, and those who manifest fleshly evil will not inherit the kingdom of God. These scriptures from Galatians enlighten us as to how Satan manifests the works of the flesh.

> Now the works of the flesh are manifest, which are these; adultery, fornication, uncleanness, lasciviousness. Idolatry, witchcraft, hatred, variance, emulations, wrath, strife, seditions, heresies, envying, murders, drunkenness, revellings and such like: of the which I tell you before, as I have also told you in time past, that they which do such things shall not inherit the kingdom of God.
>
> Galatians 5:19–21

These manifestations of the flesh sum up most of the evil in this world! Satan uses our flesh to tempt us with lust, whether sexual or material. Greed, which makes us idolize the material rather than God. Witchcraft, which is exclusively of Satan. Hatred, which is bred from contentions and arguments leading us straight to anger issues. Jealousies and self-ambitions rather than letting God lead our lives. Envying those that have more than us. The sinful act of murder. Drunkenness, regardless of which drink or drug you choose to alter your conscience. These are all ways Satan binds the flesh, and they are the root causes of temptations and spiritual warfare.

Once we accept Jesus Christ as our Lord and Savior, our salvation should bear the fruits of the Holy Spirit as we change our conduct and attitude regarding worldly things. We must die to our flesh daily and rise to the new creation that we are in Christ, therefore standing true and holy before God. Ephesians 4:22–24 helps us understand that we are to "put off concerning the former conversation the old man, which is corrupt according to the deceitful lusts; and be renewed in the spirit of your mind; And that ye put on the new man, which after God is created in righteousness and true holiness."

The word *conversation* means conduct, which helps us to understand what God is saying to us. He is telling us when we accept him we are to change our conduct.

Dying to the flesh and being reborn in the Spirit and likeness of Christ—that is what baptism symbolizes. When we accept Christ as our Savior, baptism is the way we publicly demonstrate our belief that Jesus is Lord. We die to the old man, or flesh, and rise to the new man or Spirit. Baptism does not save us; rather, it makes our profession of faith public.

Furthermore, Ephesians 4:22–24 tells us to "put off" the former conduct, which was our sin nature, and "put on" "righteousness and true holiness." Once we have God's true holiness, we are no longer enslaved to our flesh but walk in the Spirit and likeness of Christ. That is why God's children no longer have the desire to be in the flesh, but rather to be pleasing unto God in the Spirit. When we walk in righteousness before God, we are better equipped for the daily battles of spiritual warfare.

Other strongholds that have to be pulled down are lying, stealing, anger, and bitterness. Ephesians 5:2 instructs us to "walk in love, as Christ also hath loved us, and hath given himself for us an offering and a sacrifice to God for a sweet smelling savour." And Ephesians 4:25–32 teaches us how to show love to others, even our enemies, just as Christ shows love for us. To be effective in the battle of spiritual warfare, we must follow the instructions given in Ephesians 4:25–32, regardless of our circumstances.

Wherefore putting away lying, speak every man truth with his neighbour: for we are members one of another. Be ye angry, and sin not: let not the sun go down upon your wrath: Neither give place to the devil. Let him that stole steal no more: but rather let him labour, working with his hands the thing which is good, that he may have to give to him that needeth. Let no corrupt communication proceed out of your mouth, but that which is good to the use of edifying, that it may minister grace unto the hearers. And grieve not the Holy Spirit of God, whereby ye are sealed unto the day of redemption. Let all bitterness, and wrath, and anger, and clamour, and evil speaking, be put away from you, with all malice: And be ye kind one to another, tenderhearted, forgiving one another, even as God for Christ's sake hath forgiven you.

Ephesians 4:25–32

Satan knows these strongholds grieve the Holy Spirit because they hinder our faith and cripple our Christian walk. We might find it easy to not murder, steal, or lie. But how many of us refuse to forgive and allow Satan to bind us through bitterness? We cannot bear the fruits of the Spirit when we are bound by Satan's strongholds.

As Christians, we win more battles when we understand Satan, and as we stand in victory with Christ, the fruits of the Spirit begin to reveal themselves in our lives. We "put off'" more of our worldly ways and "put on" righteousness and holiness. Galatians 5:22 teaches us about the fruits of the Spirit.

> But the fruit of the Spirit is love, joy, peace, longsuffering, gentleness, goodness, faith, meekness, temperance: against such there is no law. And they that are Christ's have crucified the flesh with the affections and lusts. If we live in the Spirit, let us also walk in the Spirit. Let us not be desirous of vain glory, provoking one another, envying one another.
>
> Galatians 5:22

As new creations in Christ, we should display proper affection through a pure heart and show compassion, empathy, and understanding. We should be longsuffering, which means patient, gentle, good, and kind; be humble but not weak. We should be steady in our temperament and maintain self-control rather than to allow ourselves to be provoked to anger. Our faith in God should be apparent because our lifestyle will incorporate him in everything we do. We will have nothing to hide because we are led by the Holy Spirit and we walk in the Spirit. We should die to our flesh daily because this is the reflection of the new man.

I am not saying that we will not be tempted by Satan in an effort to make us fall back into our old worldly ways, but if we do, the Holy Spirit will be there to convict us to return to Christ. We are sealed with the Holy Spirit when we accept Christ as our Lord and Savior. There is not one Christian capable of a perfect spiritual walk. Some get close, but Satan and the flesh are always there to tempt us. These are the spiritual battles that are fought for us every day in the heavens. That is why it is so important for us to help the angels by putting on our armor of God and dying to our flesh. Satan has little to work with when we are properly protected. However, his goal is to find any minute crack in our armor in an attempt to ooze his poison into our souls and revive the flesh. That is how we get romanced back into the world by Satan.

Because Satan is such an excellent romancer of the flesh, we must daily submit ourselves to God and resist the devil. We cannot be of two minds when it comes to our spiritual walk. We cannot have one foot in Satan's world and the other foot in God's world. Only when we repent and wash our hands from the world are our hearts purified in Christ. James 4:7 reads, "Submit yourselves therefore to God. Resist the devil and he will flee from you. Draw nigh to God, and He will draw nigh to you. Cleanse your hands, ye sinners; and purify your hearts, ye double minded." The closer we walk with God, the easier it is for us to recognize Satan's temptations, and recognizing temptations helps us to circumvent and/or win spiritual battles. Therefore, we are to "have no fellowship with the unfruitful works of darkness, but rather reprove them" (Ephesians 5:11). Well, there we have it! God's Holy Word is plainly telling us not to fellowship with workers of darkness, meaning Satan and his pawns, but to expose them.

As God's children, we are to have Christlike behavior, never forgetting God gave his only Son, Jesus, to die for our sins so that we may be free from eternal death and Satan's snares. We are to walk in love and offer ourselves as a daily sacrifice to God and welcome his will in our lives. That is how we will be a sweet-smelling aroma unto him. The flesh stinks, but the Spirit is sweet.

God has enlightened us through his Holy Word about spiritual warfare, but be assured that Satan has many more tools that he uses against us. It is important for us to remember we do not fight against the actual materialism of the world but rather the temptations of the world that Satan sets before us, which causes the conflict between the flesh and the Spirit. Our flesh is daily temptation orchestrated by Satan, and that is why we must protect ourselves with the armor of God and die to our flesh. On any given day at any moment, just look up and know God has his warrior angels fighting for you right above your head. Stay vigilant, stay close to God, and maintain your victory over Satan by winning your own personal spiritual battles with God's help.

Share with God what you have learned about spiritual warfare and how to prepare yourself for the battles against Satan and his temptations.

Dear God, this is what I have learned about spiritual warfare:

Is to always put on the whole Armour of God. To always watch and pray matthew 26:41

Dear God, this is how I will prepare myself to battle Satan and the temptations he sets before me:

I will always pray and stay seeking your face, stay focus and try to always think on Good things Phill 4:8

Satan's Tools

Now that we know spiritual warfare happens daily, we need to learn how to recognize the many tools Satan uses against us in his quest to bind us. His arsenal of weapons is vast, and his army of dominions is great. Satan uses physical, mental, emotional, and spiritual weapons against us. Often, we do not see him coming until it is too late! We must remember that he roams the earth seeking those he can devour. He thrives in worldly environments and sets graceful traps to snare God's children. Satan uses every means possible to thwart God's plan for our lives. Not one person, not one event in the life of God's children is sacred to Satan. If allowed, he can transform the most precious moments into chaos! His arsenal of weapons is comprehensive, well stocked with pain, confusion, mistrust, anger, molestations, murders, pillage, drunkenness deceit, and gossip.

Satan also uses people, including Christians, to do his evil work for him. These wicked men and women come in many forms. Nonbelievers are those who reject Christ. Lip-service Christians are those who confess salvation but bear no fruits of the Spirit. Lukewarm Christians are those who attend church but never do anything to further God's kingdom. And backsliders are those who received the gift of salvation but have fallen to Satan's temptations and have returned to their worldly ways. All of *us* fall subject to being used by Satan.

Now that we understand clearly that Satan uses *everyone,* we must look beyond the human element in order to recognize the great manipulator—Satan. Earlier, we learned that Satan is our only enemy. He is the driving force behind all evil! The interesting thing is, if we allow him, he can bind us spiritually and prevent us from seeing him as the conductor or instructor of the situation or circumstance we find ourselves facing.

There are many ways we are tempted to enter into sin. Almost every element of life holds a key to the door of temptation. These keys, however subtle, have the ability to unlock the door of immediate or future chaos for us. Although Satan's tools are vast, there are eleven tools that Satan repeatedly used against me during my years of abuse. No matter how many times I slammed the door in his face, he found a way to reinsert the key in my personal door of temptation, and I let him back in!

Therefore, it is important for us to be able to recognize Satan's tools to avoid his reentry into our lives time and again. The eleven tools we will learn to discern where abuse is concerned are:

- Control

- Emotional crises

- Mental anguish

- Financial bondage

- Greed

- Pride

- Vanity

- Sexual bondage

- Physical abuse

- Verbal abuse

- Spiritual weakness

Control

"Be not deceived: evil communications corrupt good manners" (1 Corinthians 15:33).

Webster's Dictionary defines control as "to be in charge of; to maintain; to have a firm grip." While some forms of control may be productive or good, for example, a tower controller communicating with an airline pilot or a train conductor, other forms of control are very unhealthy.

Control becomes unhealthy or bad when we have fearful submission to sinful behavior; for example, bars, drugs, abortion, illegal activity, sexual promiscuity, gangs, a controlling partner, etc. These controlled settings do not allow us to think independently. We are not invited or allowed to help make important decisions that will ultimately impact our life. This creates feelings of unworthiness, which causes us to lose our self-respect. The end result for the one being controlled often leads to a lowering of self-standards, forfeiture of manners, and we often begin to mimic our controller's bad habits.

Satan tricks us into allowing ourselves to be controlled through lies and deceit, instilling fear of losing worldly things like our friends or lifestyle. He convinces us not to trust anyone, even God. As God's children, we are not to be deceived by those who speak evil. We can remove ourselves from this temptation by not hanging out with bad company. Typically, we do what everyone around us is doing, especially if *we are trying to fit in.* If we hang out with the wrong people long enough, we may find ourselves so tightly ensnared we fear removing ourselves from the situation or relationship. This is especially true about gangs. Some gangs will kill you if you do not do what they expect you to do, and they do not care if it is illegal or not! This is control in the purest form.

Another form of control can be through personal relationships. If you meet someone and you allow him or her to take control of you, he or she can rule and ruin your life. It is easy to be deceived by the subtle ways of Satan. He tries to convince us we are imaging things, or he will manipulate us into denial. I can remember my parents or friends trying to warn me about someone, but I refused to see the truth. I was blinded by Satan's lies and unable to see the truth because I did not seek God's will for my life. I refused to look beyond the human element; therefore, I was not spared the future turmoil that the bad relationship ultimately brought.

I am not the only one that has ever had to learn things the hard way. I now understand that often those around us or closest to us see things more clearly than we do. Perhaps we should listen to good advice! A controlling relationship is not what God intends for us. He did not create man to control woman or woman to control man. He created us to be equals, to complete one another, to edify and encourage, to love one another, to serve one another, to be kind, gentle, and compassionate toward one another, to speak the truth in love, and to have God's unmistakable peace in every aspect of our lives together.

Satan's deceit can never give us these things of God. To be controlled or to control another is not a spiritual trait. Avoid the wicked men and women of the world that lay in wait for you. Be vigilant, be sober, draw nigh unto God and follow him. He is the only one that has the best of life in store for you. But remember, God will never force you to do anything, so continue to seek his will in your life through prayer. Then listen and be obedient to him. I can personally assure you that if you do, he will never lead you wrong or disappoint you because life is wonderful when God is at the helm.

Emotional Crisis

"My heart is sore pained within me: and the terrors of death are fallen upon me" (Psalm 55:4).

"Woe is me for my hurt! My wound is grievous: but I said, truly this is a grief, and I must bear it" (Jeremiah 10:19).

Many times our hearts get hurt when we fall for Satan's lies, and he delights each time we feel as if our hearts are going to burst from the pain and anguish we are experiencing.

Few, if any, escape Satan's snare their entire life. Have you ever hurt so badly that you wanted to die? I have! I actually prayed to die. But God knew that was not the answer to my emotional problems. My emotional problems ran deep within my soul, spirit, and mind. It flowed freely through my veins, carried by the currents of Satan's lies as his horrid disease of deceit filled my heart. Oh, the agony of defeat! The gross miscalculations of my flesh were puny in their effort to secure a better life for myself—the undeniable lust, the greed, the frenzy of success, the whimsical melody of chance—and the end result was my wretched, torrid, miserable self. I was caught in a cesspool of swirling emotions that drug me down into the pit of utter disgust, loneliness, and despair, which was created by my own hand with Satan as my guide.

The beauty of seeking God's will and being obedient to it is that we know we are experiencing godly emotions when we feel happy, joyous, peaceful, and content. John 10:10 tells us that Satan comes as the thief to kill, steal, and destroy. Knowing this, we should be able to recognize when we are experiencing Satan's emotions because we feel confused, depressed, uncertain, fearful, and angry. All negative emotions ultimately boil down to a lack of faith and our personal inability to trust God for his leadership and the things he has promised us in his Holy Word.

There are many events that cause us to become emotional—death, finances, getting married, unstable relationships, the birth of a child, moving, job issues, hurt feelings, etc. However, it is imperative that we remember God is not the author of confusion! If we seek God's will for every aspect of our lives, he will be faithful to comfort and lead us.

But when we reject God by not seeking his will or blatantly refusing to be obedient, we open ourselves up for Satan's strongholds. Satan seizes every opportunity he can find to whisper his lies in our ears, trying to make us falter in our faith. He knows how difficult it is for us to let go of emotional distress. This is why he uses it as one of his greatest tools against us.

Lingering emotional distress ultimately transforms into mental anguish. Prolonged periods of emotional distress can also trigger physical illnesses. We would be much healthier if we believed in and trusted God for everything like we are supposed to, according to the Scriptures.

Mental Anguish

"Because the carnal mind is enmity against God; for it is not subject to the law of God, neither indeed can be. So then they that are in the flesh cannot please God" (Romans 8:7–8).

Mental anguish is one of Satan's favorite weapons because it can last for years! Mental anguish is a "sustained dull painful emotion," according to Webster's Dictionary. Following are a few examples of mental anguish:

- Inability or unwillingness to forgive someone of a wrong

- Unable to accept the death of a loved one

- Unable to accept permanent physical conditions

- Wounded hearts by verbal or physical abuse

This weapon of Satan's can keep you chained in your flesh for many years, because he can control your mind when you are not focused on God. That is why we should always draw nigh unto God and keep him in our hearts and minds. Satan has to flee when we walk in the Holy Spirit.

Earlier, we learned that carnal means flesh, so to paraphrase Romans 8:7–8, *a mind filled with the thoughts of the flesh is an enmity mind and is not of God. Because it is not of God, it is not subject to God's law but dwells in Satan's pit, and anyone in the pit cannot please God.* I believe that is why some people try to control others mentally. They use harsh words and actions to beat down their victims, causing them to suffer mental fatigue and distress. Once they have broken down, they can brainwash them into believing just about anything, and Satan loves it when we dwell in his pit!

We know Romans 8:7–8 applies to the unsaved, but does it not also apply to the saved when they allow Satan to control their minds through mental anguish? Christians can also dwell in the flesh mentally and not even realize they are bound!

The Bible tells us we cannot serve two masters; either we serve God or Satan. If we choose to serve Satan, our minds are carnal and ensnared with the flesh. Our empty minds open the door for Satan to bind us through mental anguish.

The wonderful news is that we do not have to remain bound by mental anguish! We can lose this stronghold and avoid future mental anguish by:

- Preparing ourselves for battle daily by putting on our armor of God

- Forgiving those who trespass and sin against us

- Accepting the things we cannot change

- Believing that God is in control at all times and he has our best interest at heart

So when we start to feel those bad or raw emotions creeping up on us, we need to call on Jesus, and he will cause Satan to flee from us!

Financial Bondage

> "But Peter said unto him, thy money perish with thee, because thou hast thought that the gift of God may be purchased with money" (Acts 8:20).

> "For the love of money is the root of all evil; which while some coveted after, they have erred from the faith, and pierced themselves through with money sorrows" (1 Timothy 6:10).

Peter makes it abundantly clear that we cannot purchase God's gift of salvation with money and that we will never be able to buy our way into heaven. Money is man's material wealth, not spiritual wealth. We will not take any material wealth we have collected with us when we die, no matter how much we hold on to it in the here and now. Once we die, our earthly possessions are rendered useless to us. The inheritance may be left to loved ones, but for us it is simply over from a materialistic, earthly perspective. But do not be fooled; it may be over for us on earth, but our eternity is just beginning, and if we put the love for money before God, our money will perish with us, and instead of eternal life we will receive eternal torment and damnation. First Timothy 6:10 points out the root of all evil is the *love* of money, and with that comes money sorrows. Satan will use anything and everyone he can to snare you financially. He would have us believe that money will buy us everything we need. According to Satan:

- Money will buy us happiness! *Wrong*

- Money will buy us love! *Wrong*

- Money will buy us health! *Wrong*

The only thing money can buy us are sorrows! Satan tempts us to go in debt for more than we can afford. He tempts us to live beyond our means, and then when we are over our heads in debt, he sits back and laughs at us!

We must be good stewards of the financial blessings that God allows us and use our blessings to help those who are in need and to further his kingdom. I am not saying that we are supposed to live like paupers for the Lord. However, I am saying that we should follow biblical principles and give God his 10 percent off the top. If we are faithful to tithe according to the Scriptures, then he will be faithful to continue to bless us.

So the next time you want to purchase an item that is beyond your financial means, do not let Satan woo you into doing something you will regret later. The money sorrows begin when the payment coupon book arrives and you realize that you are in over your head financially!

Another way Satan places financial strongholds is by using those we care about. Be careful when it comes to lending money or repeatedly bailing someone out of his or her financial crises, especially when he or she has created the crises knowing that you will come to his or her financial rescue. Friends and family members often know our weaknesses and use them against us for their own financial gain. Do not allow Satan to make you feel guilty when enough is enough! Granted, there are times when we should help those who are truly in need, but you should make certain that by helping them financially, you are not aiding them in their own self-destruction.

Satan has many ways to financially bind us. He often sends people who offer us deals that we cannot refuse! Before venturing into any business partnerships or lending someone money to start a business, thoroughly check out the person, his or her work ethics, and the business idea before committing to him or her financially. We should always follow the principle that if it sounds too good to be true, it usually is. Satan sets no boundaries, and he uses very cunning and clever people to do his evil business transactions. Do not allow yourself to fall victim to one of his scams!

Greed

> "So are the ways of everyone that is greedy of gain; which taketh away the life of the owners thereof" (Proverbs 1:19).

This proverb is confirming that those who are greedy use any means possible to achieve financial gain. Often, they ruin their own lives finically, as well as the lives of those they manipulated along the way. Greedy people typically do not care who they mow over on the way to their coveted jackpot; all they can see is the fake gold at the end of the rainbow. My, how Satan uses fool's gold to snare so many. As God's children, if we stay close to him and seek his will in our lives through prayer, he will show us the difference between fool's gold and spiritual rewards.

On the other hand, we should not be so greedy or stingy that we never live life to the fullest. Those around us do not recognize us as Christians when we are greedy. We do not bear spiritual fruit when the roots of our soul are planted in the evil soil of greed! Greed makes us miserable, those around us miserable, or both.

Once again, we cannot take our earthly wealth with us when we die, so we should use our financial blessings to help those who are truly in need and to further the kingdom of God. According to Matthew 6:20, we should lay up for ourselves heavenly treasures: "But lay up for yourselves treasures in heaven, where neither moth nor rust doth corrupt, and where thieves do not break through nor steal." Our heavenly treasures will be with us for all eternity, and we will be pleasing unto God for the way we handled the financial blessings he bestowed upon us while on earth.

Pride

> "For all that is in the world, the lust of the flesh, and the lust of the eyes, and the pride of life, is not of the Father, but is of the world" (1 John 2:16).

One definition of pride is a high opinion of one's own importance or superiority, whether in the mind or displayed in conduct (www.dictionary.com).

Pride is created when we lust after worldly items in the flesh, and our flesh will eventually fail us, and we will fall from grace. Because our lust is driven by Satan, the things we look upon with our eyes and lust after in our hearts ultimately come full circle to selfish greed, which requires money to purchase, which is the root of all evil. Like a cat chasing its tail, Satan uses pride as a vicious circle or cycle to manipulate us into believing his lies.

The Bible tells us Satan's failure as ultimate ruler is certain and those that follow him into eternity will suffer with him. First John 2:16 confirms why we should be careful not to lust after material wealth or physical superiority. We should be good stewards because the Bible instructs us to be financially responsible and to care for our earthy vessel or body. We should never put the world and its earthly treasures before God, who created it! Everything belongs to him anyway!

Genesis tells us God created everything, including man and woman, to whom he imparted intelligence and skills to live upon and work the earth. Now, in my simple reasoning, if God created it, then it is ultimately his, and we should ask him for his blessings and not just take for granted that we can do whatever we want with his creation.

Of course, Satan would have us believe that we should not have to ask God for anything. However, out of love and respect for our creator, we should seek his will in our lives and ask him for everything! Let me explain it this way. How would you like it if I waltzed into your house with my big ole shopping bags and started helping myself to whatever you had and did not even bother to ask you about it, much less say please and thank you? I'm certain God is treated that way by humans each moment of every day. How audacious of us to behave like that. The reason most people will not or simply do not ask God for his blessings is *pride.*

Satan likes to make us think we do not have to ask anyone for anything, including God. But as usual, he is wrong. Our pride keeps us from doing the right thing by our Lord and Savior. This is why we should always pray for God's will to be done in our lives and make our request through the name of Jesus Christ. We certainly have the authority to go before the throne of God personally, which is what the tearing of the veil was all about when Christ was crucified at Calvary. Are you aware that before Christ died to pay for our sins, the throne of God could only be approached by a high priest, and a pure blood sacrifice had to be made prior to the priest entering the holy room? Not only that, if you had a request for God, you had to give it to the priest and he asked God for it on your behalf.

I am so glad to be a Christian on the post side of the Cross. Jesus Christ was the pure blood sacrifice that set down the new covenant so we might personally approach the throne of God. That is why we close our prayers with "in the name of Jesus, we pray." Jesus Christ *is* our high priest, and his precious and pure blood was shed once for all of us sinners. Knowing that, how can we not desire to ask God for his blessings instead of taking them for granted?

God loves his children! We should not have a problem with setting our selfish pride aside and kneeling before him in prayerful petition. Sometimes it may feel like he is not answering your prayers, but patience will reveal God's blessing for your life. Do not lean on your own pride, but instead pray in faith and be patient, then watch how marvelous God's blessings will be. Do not let Satan's tool of pride stand in the way of your blessings.

Vanity

> "For when they speak great swelling words of vanity, they allure through the lusts of the flesh, through much wantonness, those that were clean escaped from them who live in error" (2 Peter 2:18).

How many times are we taken in by the smooth talkers, speaking "great swelling words of vanity," alluring us "through the lusts of the flesh"? Guilty as charged, your honorable Lord. Many times, we fall for the smooth lies and grab hold of the flesh with "much wantonness," refusing to see the truth of the matter. We are too busy paying homage to our vanity and swallow the compliments of impending catastrophe with great pride.

We often neglect our spiritual ears when someone makes us feel good about ourselves. All compliments are not of Satan, but the smooth talkers with the satin tongues usually have an ultimate goal in mind, and if we fall victim to them, they turn out to be bad for us! Only God can implant a spiritual hearing aide so we may hear clearly their "swelling words of vanity."

It is amazing how many people actually portray their vanity. The last part of the scripture instructs the righteous on how to deal with those who are unclean with their tongue, "those that were clean escaped from them who live in error." Praise God, I am an escapee, and you can be one too!

Vanity comes in many forms: beauty, cars, houses, clothes, social status, job titles, etc. I personally feel vanity and shallowness go hand in hand. My parents used to tell me, "Do not break your arm patting yourself on the back." Thanks to their lack of vanity, they taught me that compliments are to be given to others and received from others, not reserved for you, or to be spoken by you on behalf of yourself. It is all right to be complimented by others for a job well done or a game well played. And it is okay to feel proud of an accomplishment. But we are to accept the compliments and accolades with humbleness and gracefulness. These types of compliments are not considered "swelling words of vanity." It is important for us to understand the difference between true heartfelt compliments and false or deceitful statements made to create a calculated reaction to a particular situation. In other words, to be manipulated! Vanity can be played both ways—by the speaker and the hearer. It truly is a double dragon tool! Do not be lured by their vanity and do not fall victim to yours. Escape from Satan's snare and live amongst the clean that are also known as the righteous.

Sexual Bondage

> "But every man is tempted, when he is drawn away of his own lust, and enticed. Then when lust hath conceived, it bringeth forth sin: and sin, when it is finished, bringeth forth death" (James 1:14–15).

Lust is a multifaceted tool, and there are many ways Satan tempts us with it. Most people associate the word lust with sex, and in some instances that is a very appropriate interpretation of the word. Satan uses sexual bondage to control many people. It is a fierce weapon, and it is amazing how many people fall victim to it. There have been great men of stature that have fallen because of sexual bondage, and there have been many average men and women who have fallen to sexual bondage. The fact is Satan does not care if we are people of notoriety or not. His main goal is to hold us and keep us weak in our faith. Satan tempts us or draws us to our sexual lust through:

- Pornography via the Internet, magazines, or movies

- Promiscuous behavior

- Prudish behavior, which is also a form of sexual bondage

- Hiring escort services and prostitutes

- Cult leaders sleeping with the girls and women

- Gangs sexually initiating women and sometimes men

- Homosexuality

- Dressing provocatively

We often bring sexual bondage on ourselves by the way we present ourselves to others, either through provocative attire or flirtatious behavior, or both. The way we dress speaks volumes about what we are looking for. When I was in my twenties and thirties, it made me mad when men looked at me dripping with desire and made crude sexual comments to me. It never occurred to me to look in the mirror! I felt I had the right to wear anything I wanted to, no matter how revealing, and not be bothered by people. It was my right as a woman to display my body the way I wished without repercussion. I see now how foolish I was. Not only was I sending out signals that I was a promiscuous person, I was literally inviting Satan's pawns into my world. We must understand that Satan knows no boundaries, so when we willingly enter his lust zone, we are putting ourselves directly in harm's way. Granted, there are heinous crimes of passion committed every minute that have absolutely nothing to do with how someone is dressed. Some suffer the consequences of others sins for no apparent reason other than sin and sin alone.

Once we receive Christ as our Lord and Savior and are reborn to his likeness, the Holy Spirit convicts us to be conscious of our outward appearance. Our profession of salvation does not count for much when we are still dressing provocatively. I found it hard to profess God while standing in a mini skirt and halter top! That is when I realized if I were going to talk the talk, I truly had to walk the walk, and that included my outward appearance. Needless to say, my wardrobe began to change, and my spiritual walk grew by leaps and bounds.

We can still look pleasing and not emit all the wrong signals associated with sexual prowess. God grew me immensely and showed me how my own choices in my outward appearance attracted or rejected Satan's pawns. When we dress like a child of God, more people treat us with respect, and we seldom suffer crude remarks. In addition, we feel better about ourselves because we are clothed outwardly and inwardly in righteousness! We should present ourselves to the world as a walking reflection of God.

Other ways we can remain free from sexual bondage are to:

- Abstain from any and all sexual behavior outside of the covenant of marriage, which is between a man and a woman

- Educate our children about sexual boundaries

- Teach our children about God's expectations of purity

- Educate our children about sexual predators

Sexual bondage comes in many forms and takes on many names. Satan may try to bind us, and in some cases he succeeds, but God never wants us to be bound. All we have to do is repent and turn from our sin, and God will replace Satan's bondage with his purity.

Physical Abuse

"Remove thy stroke away from me: I am consumed by the blow of thine hand" (Psalm 39:10).

Satan uses his pawns to inflict physical abuse on others, especially spouses and children. Psalm 39:10 is actually referencing a plague that God sent down to punish the sinners, but it can be used to illustrate that no one *except God* has the right to strike a blow, meaning to discipline his children for their sins. This does not include bringing your children up with the appropriate balance of love and discipline. Proverbs 13:24 tells us, "He that spareth his rod hateth his son: but he that loveth him chasteneth him betimes." In simple language, parents are called to discipline their children on occasion if their behavior merits it. However, beating or inappropriate discipline is completely unacceptable to God. That is why God punishes those who continue to sin mightily against him, but he does not look kindly upon anyone who causes his children to suffer, *children* meaning young in age and those who have accepted Christ as their Lord and Savior. Satan uses physical abuse to subdue and control. Even God's children can fall victim to Satan through the terror of physical abuse.

To be maliciously hit by the hand of a relative, co-worker, friend, enemy, or stranger has absolutely no place in our lives. There is not one reason that a person should suffer rape, molestation, or physical abuse. It does not matter how angry you or they get; physical abuse is not the answer!

If you or anyone you know is suffering physical abuse, I encourage you and/or her to remove yourself and/or herself from the abusive environment, even if it means seeking safety at a women's shelter, and seek God's will for your life. God has the right answers, and he will supply the strength that is needed to make the necessary changes in your and/or her life.

I personally know how difficult it is to escape from physical abuse and the emotional upset of being beaten by a mean-spirited individual or a drunk or drugged fool who is telling you what an awful person you are with every blow! The effects of the abuse leaves you withered and shrunken in your spirit, mind, body, and soul as you crumple to a crying heap of nothingness on the floor, waiting for the raging storm of pain and torment to cease. Then, frail and timid, you manage to reclaim a small portion of yourself, however bruised and battered, and try to put the puzzle of life back together again. You tell yourself this is the last time it will ever happen, believing the lie time and again. What type of existence is this? A miserable one with Satan at the helm! But I know something beautiful; God *will* deliver you from Satan's snare. God did not create us to be Satan's whipping post, and he does not expect us to live in an abusive environment. You must flee from Satan! You can do this through faith and by asking God to show you his way; then believe and obey his instructions. That is news worth sharing! So once again, I urge you to share God with anyone you may know who is suffering abuse. God will bless you and them for it! You might even want to encourage them walk their own personal journey of courage to find complete healing through Jesus Christ.

Verbal Abuse

"His mouth is full of cursing and deceit and fraud: under his tongue is mischief and vanity" (Psalm 10:7).

I have found most people that curse regularly struggle to be positive. It is my opinion that cursing is generally associated with displeasure and is typically revealed by taking the Lord's name in vain. Of course, there are those who curse because they think it makes them sound tough or cool, or they mimic the vocabulary of their family, friends, or co-workers. You cannot be a child of God and curse the Lord with a vile tongue.

Furthermore, if a person has so much displeasure in his or her life, his or her outlook is often skewed, and the truth is lost somewhere in the battle between what is right and what is wrong. Fraud and slander go hand in hand. We often put a spin on something someone else said and present it to another person totally different than it was originally meant to be. How deceitful is the person twisting the words and how terrible the end result can be! Also, relationships can be damaged because of fraudulent words spoken in deceit. Many people never make right their wrongful statements even when they see the damages their words have caused. Very few people get past their pride enough to admit they were wrong and offer an apology to the offended.

Because verbal abuse comes in many forms, we should never allow Satan to use us for his treacherous gossip. Foul and harsh words are often used in an effort to control and subdue. Even Christians can inflict verbal abuse on friends, loved ones, and especially strangers. The next time you are in a long checkout line, pay attention to the behavior of the people in front of you. You might be amazed how verbally rude the people around you are. Bless the cashiers and store associates that receive the brunt of society's verbal abuse. Typically, the problem was not created by the employees, but the backlash of the issue is received by them from every irritated or angry person just waiting for his or her turn to vent.

Perhaps you have had a bad day and a family member comes home from work, school, or errands; and as soon as he or she walks through the door, you verbally assault him or her for no apparent reason. At least, not one he or she can comprehend, because in reality all he or she did was come home. Then the battle is on, and what could have been a peaceful evening spent *discussing* the irritating issues of the day turns into an argument. And it all started verbally! Nothing good ever comes from a vile tongue, and a vile tongue is always driven by Satan!

As Christians, we should have a new perspective on how to present ourselves privately and publicly in all situations. We should see with spiritual eyes and hear with spiritual ears, because when we view the world through the eyes and heart of Christ, it becomes a very different world. If you find yourself in a verbally abusive situation, you should politely ask the person to refrain from the assault or simply turn and walk away from the confrontation. Otherwise, you are allowing Satan to bind you, and your behavior does not depict Christ. Write Psalm 10:7 upon your heart and do not allow Satan to turn your tongue into a vile instrument of verbal destruction.

Spiritual Weakness

> "And he said unto me, My grace is sufficient for thee: for my strength is made perfect in weakness. Most gladly therefore will I rather glory in my infirmities, that the power of Christ may rest upon me" (2 Corinthians 12:9).

The ten strongholds we have previously discussed all play a major role in tearing down our faith, and Satan uses them to bind us with spiritual weakness. Although control, emotions, mental anguish, financial bondage, greed, pride, vanity, sexual bondage, and physical and verbal abuse cause us to falter in our flesh, 2 Corinthians 12:9 reassures us that our weaknesses may be made strong through Christ and also encourages us to rely on the Lord's grace because it is sufficient.

Human weakness can be physical, mental, and/or emotional, or a combination of many weaknesses. Satan knows if he can cause us to stumble in our faith, our spiritual eyes and ears close and we no longer see God's truth.

As Christians, we should understand that Satan knows our weaknesses, because Ephesians 6:12 tells us that we wrestle not against the flesh but with the rulers of the darkness of this world and against spiritual wickedness in high places.

It may feel like we are wrestling with the flesh, but if we spiritually look behind the human conflict we are facing, there is only one entity standing there wielding his evil weapons of destruction, and his name is *Satan.*

Following are several ways Satan binds us spiritually and weakens our faith:

- He hinders our prayer life

- He encourages us to sin by tempting us with worldly things

- He hinders our Christian walk

- He attacks us physically to hinder God's work

- He causes conflict in the churches

- He causes conflict at home, school, and at work

- He causes conflict in our country via wars, rumors of wars, and economical issues

Despite Satan's greatest attempts to make us stumble, we can avoid falling into his pit of spiritual weakness by doing the following:

- We should pray, draw nigh unto God, and seek his will for our lives

- We should fellowship with godly people and avoid worldly environments

- We should read the Bible regularly and/or do daily devotionals

- We should go to Sunday school and church every week

- We should participate in Bible studies at church or on our own

- We should minister to those who are in need

- We should share the love of Christ and the gift of salvation with others

Because Satan is always on the prowl, seeking whom he may devour, we should put on these five spiritual items found in Ephesians chapter 6 as part of our daily wardrobe:

- The helmet of salvation

- The breastplate of righteousness

- The belt of truth

- Our sword and shield (which is the Holy Bible)

- The shoes of the gospel

God teaches us everything we need to know about preparing ourselves for our daily battles in order to avoid spiritual weakness. This preparation also includes learning to distinguish the difference between spiritual fruit and worldly fruit, which we will cover in "Be A Fruit Inspector." It is up to us to follow God's instructions and to protect ourselves from Satan's strongholds. We should always stand in Ephesians chapter 6 and be prepared to stand victorious with Christ.

Now that we understand more about how Satan uses everyday life as a weapon of spiritual destruction, take time to reflect on your life. Identify the tools he has used to stronghold you in the past and the tools he uses to stronghold you now. Then define the changes you should make in your life to avoid future strongholds.

These are the tools Satan used to stronghold me in the past:

_____

_____

_____

_____

_____

These are the tools Satan uses to stronghold me now:

_____

_____

_____

_____

These are the changes I should make to avoid future strongholds:

_____

_____

_____

_____

Be a Fruit Inspector

Once we realize how Satan works, it is easier to recognize his evil and sneaky ways. Also, when our spiritual eyes and ears are open, we are able to discern the difference between those who bear spiritual fruit and those who bear the fruits of the world.

Because Satan deceives us in so many ways, we must become fruit inspectors. Our inspection of one's fruit should not turn into judging; rather, it should reveal the true nature of the one being inspected and allow us spiritual discernment of his or her personality, spirituality, and motives.

Deuteronomy 22:9 tells us, "Thou shalt not sow thy vineyard with divers seeds: lest the fruit of thy seed which thoust hast sown, and the fruit of thy vineyard, be defiled." The vineyard is our life, and the diversity of seeds we sow in the world will defile our spiritual walk and expose us to Satan's attacks. This scripture applies to everyone! The unsaved sow the seeds of eternal damnation, and if we are not fruit inspectors, Satan will tempt us to join them in worldly activities.

Romans 6:21 teaches us that we will be ashamed of our worldly sins when we stand before the judgment throne of God. We can avoid this shame if we repent and turn from our worldly ways. If we do not, we will not have eternal life and our sins will end in death. "What fruit had ye then in those things whereof ye are now ashamed? For the end of those things is death."

These scriptural fruits can leave a bitter taste in your mouth if you are not a child of God. He is teaching us through his Holy Word that we will eat the bitterness of the unrighteous fruits we bear in our earthly life for all eternity unless we repent and turn from our wicked ways. The pit of hell will be a constant replay of our life and all the times we rejected Christ and chose the ways of the world.

As Christians, we cannot sow diverse seeds. We must stay focused on Christ, or Satan will find his way into our hearts to corrupt and defile us. He may even use our *friends* to deceive us and lead us astray. We must not choose the temporary pleasures and riches of the world, like putting your career before God, drinking or doing drugs, having multiple sex partners, or partying instead of going to church. These are just a few of the things of the world that seem to promise pleasure. But they never last and only lead to destruction and failures. When we bear worldly fruits, our testimony is stained with sin, and we are not effective witnesses for Christ. Our Christian walk should reveal the truths of our heart, and our harvest should be the fruits of the spirit. According to Romans 5:22–23, "The fruit of the spirit is love, joy, peace, longsuffering, gentleness, goodness, faith, meekness, temperance; against such there is no law."

We should also realize that while we are inspecting another's fruit, he or she might also be inspecting our fruits. It is important for us to understand how others perceive us and how our behavior impacts our testimony. Do your actions and social activities truly depict your salvation and the fruits of the spirit? The only way to answer this question is through self-inspection.

While it may seem easy for us to inspect another's fruit, it can be difficult for us to look at our own fruits. However, it is critical that we take the time to see ourselves as others see us. Only then will we know if we actually bear the fruits of the spirit and if our Christian walk is all that God expects it to be. Romans 6:22 assures us that our self-inspection and corrections from sin will bring us everlasting life at the end of our earthly time: "But now being made free from sin, and become servants to God, ye have your fruit unto holiness, and the end everlasting life."

God searches us according to our ways and our fruits. Now is the time to become a fruit inspector and search the ways of your family, friends, co-workers, and fellow Christians. Do not judge them; simply inspect the fruits they bear. If they are not producing spiritual fruits, then share Jesus with them and encourage them to become a child of God. Also, inspect your own fruit! Truthfully search yourself and ask God through prayer to show you how others see you and how *he* sees you. Once you recognize the changes that you need to make to bear the fruits of the spirit, share them with God and ask him to grow you spiritually.

―――――――――

These are the fruits of my family:

Name:

_____

Fruits:

_____

_____

_____

_____

_____

Name:

_____

Fruits:

_____

_____

_____

_____

_____

Name:

_____

Fruits:

_____

_____

_____

_____

_____

Name:

_____

Fruits:

_____

_____

_____

_____

Name:

_____

Fruits:

_____

_____

_____

_____

Name:

_____

Fruits:

_____

_____

_____

_____

_____

Name:

_____

Fruits:

_____

_____

_____

_____

_____

Name:

_____

Fruits:

_____

_____

_____

_____

Name:

_____

Fruits:

_____

_____

_____

_____

Name:

_____

Fruits:

_____

_____

_____

_____

Name:

_____

Fruits:

_____

_____

_____

_____

Name:

_____

Fruits:

_____

_____

_____

_____

Name:

_____

Fruits:

_____

_____

_____

_____

Name:

_____

Fruits:

_____

_____

_____

_____

Name:

_____

Fruits:

_____

_____

_____

_____

These are the fruits of my friends:

Name:

_____

Fruits:

_____

_____

_____

_____

Name:

_____

Fruits:

_____

_____

_____

_____

Name:

_____

Fruits:

_____

_____

_____

_____

Name:

_____

Fruits:

_____

_____

_____

_____

Name:

_____

Fruits:

_____

_____

_____

_____

Name:

_____

Fruits:

_____

_____

_____

_____

Name:

_____

Fruits:

_____

_____

_____

_____

_____

Name:

_____

Fruits:

_____

_____

_____

_____

_____

Name:

_____

Fruits:

_____

_____

_____

_____

_____

Name:

_____

Fruits:

_____

_____

_____

_____

_____

―――――――――

These are the fruits of my co-workers:

Name:

_____

Fruits:

_____

_____

_____

_____

_____

Name:

_____

Fruits:

_____

_____

_____

_____

_____

Name:

_____

Fruits:

_____

_____

_____

_____

Name:

_____

Fruits:

_____

_____

_____

_____

Name:

_____

Fruits:

_____

_____

_____

_____

_____

Name:

_____

Fruits:

_____

_____

_____

_____

_____

Name:

_____

Fruits:

_____

_____

_____

_____

_____

Name:

_____

Fruits:

_____

_____

_____

_____

_____

Name:

_____

Fruits:

_____

_____

_____

_____

Name:

_____

Fruits:

_____

_____

_____

_____

_____

These are the fruits of the Spirit I am weak in, and these are the changes that I need to make so others will see Christ in me:

Fruit:

_____

Change:

_____

_____

_____

_____

Fruit:

_____

Change:

_____

_____

_____

_____

Fruit:

_____

Change:

_____

_____

_____

_____

Fruit:

_____

Change:

_____

_____

_____

_____

Fruit:

_____

Change:

_____

_____

_____

_____

Fruit:

_____

Change:

_____

_____

_____

_____

Fruit:

_____

Change:

_____

_____

_____

_____

Fruit:

_____

Change:

_____

_____

_____

_____

_____

Fruit:

_____

Change:

_____

_____

_____

_____

_____

"The fruit of the spirit is love, joy, peace, longsuffering, gentleness, goodness, faith, meekness, temperance" (Romans 5:22–23).

Friend or Foe

I hope that your fruit inspection brought you to an understanding of how we should conduct ourselves if we proclaim to be a Christian. Furthermore, we should take the necessary measures in our lives to weed out all ungodly relationships and build new godly ones. Because of our abuse, our perception of true friendship is often skewed, and we not only enter into but develop relationships with manipulative people. We should not have friends that are against us or God, for their worldly temptations may lead us astray. James 4:4 teaches us, whoever is a friend of the world is the enemy of God; therefore, an enemy of God can never be a true friend to us.

As Christians we must embrace and surround ourselves with godly friends that have pure hearts. True friends are faithful, especially when they speak the truth to us in *love*. Sometimes honesty hurts, and only true and faithful friends love us enough to reveal those truths to us, however gently, but with great honesty. This kind of friendship strengthens or sharpens our individual countenance and confirms that a true friend will love us during the trials and tribulations of our life as well as the good times. These friends may be closer to you than your own family. The bond of Christ's heart exists in these friendships, and with the dual strength of their prayers and supplications, the wickedness of Satan can be beaten down.

Scripture tells us where two or more are gathered in Christ name, he will be in the midst: "For where two or three are gathered together in my name, there am I in the midst of them" (Matthew 18:20). If our hearts and minds are in one accord and prayerful petition is made in the name of Jesus, so shall it be: "If ye shall ask any thing in my name, I will do it" (John 14:14). How precious to have a friend and prayer warrior in Christ. True godly friendships will bear the fruits of the spirit. They will speak the truth with love. They will pray with you in times of tribulation and rejoice with you in times of joy. Jealously will not exist, nor will harsh and hurtful words be spoken, because they know it will hurt you. They will not tickle your ears with lies and lead you into temptation. They will love God the Father, Jesus Christ the Son, and invoke the Holy Spirit. This is the love and fruit of a true friend.

On the other hand, we should be wary of those that call themselves our friends yet wound us emotionally, physically, mentally, and spiritually. Micah 7:5 tells us not to trust in a friend or put confidence in a guide that claims to be a friend of the heart yet can not be trusted: "Trust ye not in a friend, put ye not confidence in a guide: keep the doors of thy mouth from her that lieth in thy bosom." He or she may shake our hand or hug our neck and pledge his or her friendship to us, but his or her intention is to control us through the friendship. This is the depiction of a foe and not a godly friend.

A foe disguised as a friend is one who always wants something from you yet never gives anything in return. He or she will be your friend as long as you are the one who always pays for the meal or buys the movie ticket. Although he or she claims to be your friend, all he or she ever does is use you. The world is full of these foes, and they are very clever with their friendly ways. But time always reveals the truth, and scripture tells us the truth will set us free.

Another foe disguised as a friend bears the worldly fruit of anger. Proverbs 22:24 instructs us to "make no friendship with an angry man; and with a furious man thou shalt not go." This is scripture worth remembering! Anger issues that cannot be controlled often become embarrassing when unsuspecting events turn into a public brawl or vile verbal assault. God has clearly taught us anger is not a fruit of the spirit, and angry people have issues deeper than you or I can deal with. God's healing power is the only way for them to heal the root cause of their anger. Often, we do not understand their angry behavior because they have hidden their secrets in the deep recesses of their heart. We as Christians should remove ourselves from this relationship if possible and pray that God would do a great work in their heart.

James 4:4 teaches us that anyone who loves the world and its ways more than God is not a friend at all. In fact, he or she is an enemy to God. These are Satan's pawns, and he uses these friendly foes to lead us into sin. If we do not remove ourselves from these relationships, we may fall to temptation and allow Satan to bind us.

It must be hard from God's perspective to watch his children be persuaded by *friends* to enter into worldly ways. Jesus shed his precious blood that we might be cleansed and free from sin, and then we turn around and succumb to peer pressure. It grieves me to know I failed Christ so many times, but it also relieves me to know I have asked for forgiveness and have been forgiven. The last thing we should allow is for deceitful friends to woo us back into Satan's web. That is why we must stand firm in our belief and live by faith. There is not one thing the world has to offer that is better than God's love and grace. The world will not be there to pick us up when we fall. Nor will it be there to comfort us and give us peace during times of tribulation. The world can never save us from the eternal pit of hell. Nor does it display the fruits of the spirit.

Beware of foes, because the world is full of Satan's dominions therein. What a difference there is between a true friend and a foe.

It is extremely important that we be able to recognize the truth about our friends, and we must have the courage to separate ourselves from foes that are disguised as friends. Take a few moments to think about the friends in your life. In chapter nine you listed their fruits of the spirit; now list the names of your friends again and describe your relationship with them to help you discern whether they are true friends or a foe in disguise. Ask God through prayer to reveal *his truths* to you before you begin.

Name:

_____

Our relationship:

_____

_____

_____

_____

_____

(Circle one) *Friend   Foe*

Name:

_____

Our relationship:

_____

_____

_____

_____

(Circle one) *Friend   Foe*

Name:

_____

Our relationship:

_____

_____

_____

_____

(Circle one) *Friend   Foe*

Name:

_____

Our relationship:

_____

_____

_____

_____

(Circle one) *Friend   Foe*

Name:

_____

Our relationship:

_____

_____

_____

_____

(Circle one) *Friend   Foe*

Name:

_____

Our relationship:

_____

_____

_____

_____

(Circle one) *Friend   Foe*

Name:

_____

Our relationship:

_____

_____

_____

_____

_____

(Circle one) *Friend   Foe*

Name:

_____

Our relationship:

_____

_____

_____

_____

(Circle one) *Friend   Foe*

Name:

_____

Our relationship:

_____

_____

_____

_____

(Circle one) *Friend   Foe*

Name:

_____

Our relationship:

_____

_____

_____

_____

_____

(Circle one) *Friend* *Foe*

Heart Under Construction

I hope you were able to see how you were, or are, manipulated at the hands of Satan and perhaps foes marauding as friends. Often we inadvertently allow these manipulations to happen after the initial abuse. We typically accept the bad things in life based on emotions and bad choices rather than following God's instructions. Were you able to see how your life was altered and swayed by others in your past and perhaps even today? It is rather hard to acknowledge such treachery. However, God loves us so much he does not want us to beat ourselves up about it. His desire is for us to recognize the ungodly things in our life, make the necessary changes, forgive others and ourselves as he forgave us, and continue to grow and heal through him. Christ teaches us how to reconstruct our hearts.

Begin reconstructing your heart to be like his, and continue to mature and grow spiritually.

The Bible teaches us through the scriptures how to maintain peace regardless of our situation if circumstances bar us from removing ourselves from the situation. As children of God, we will still go through trials and tribulations, but we will be equipped to deal with the unexpected issues of life that arise, and maintain our peace through Christ. "Let the peace of God rule in your hearts … and be ye thankful" (Colossians 3:15).

To be thankful during the storms of life, we must put on the characteristics of God and continually forgive our transgressors. We have the flesh to deal with on a daily basis. However, if we follow God's instructions and change our hearts to be like his, we will accomplish our transformation. Reconstructing your heart is an ongoing process. Daily challenges require daily changes. To have a heart like Christ, you must put on compassion, kindness, humility, gentleness, patience, forbearance, forgiveness, and love.

If we let God rule in our hearts, we will be thankful for the peace he gives us. If we hide God's Holy Word in our hearts, we will have the wisdom to distinguish friends from foes. We can deal with situations by word or by action in the name of Jesus Christ, which causes Satan to flee from us. Sounds like tough scriptures to follow, but God would not have left them for us if we could not do it with his help. It is very difficult to walk away from an argument or confrontation. However, God makes it clear in his Scripture not to return evil for evil or speak deceit.

> Not rendering evil for evil or railing for railing ... for he that will love life, and see good days, let him refrain his tongue from evil, and his lips that they speak no guile. Let him eschew evil, and do good, let him seek peace, and ensure it, for the eyes of the Lord are over the righteous, and his ears are open unto their prayers: But the face of the Lord is against them that do evil.
>
> 1 Peter 3:9–14

He also tells us if we suffer for his sake, we will be blessed. Once you understand that Satan is wielding his power over your transgressor, who is set against you, cast him behind you in the name of Jesus and refuse to be bound. Scripture also tells us not to be afraid or troubled at their threats, but to sanctify the Lord God in our hearts.

Be reassured that God will help you overcome the situation or confrontation as long as you are pure in heart and call upon his help. With reassurances like these, we have nothing to fear except *not* walking with God. Having God's mighty protection surrounding you ensures that he will be with you in your times of distress.

When responding to others, you should demonstrate compassion and be courteous. You should not react with evil to an evil situation; for example, if you are being yelled at, do not respond with yelling. You can walk by faith, persevering in your battles, provided that you have put on your armor of God and written his scriptures upon your heart. Apply the teachings that Christ left for us in his Holy Word to your daily life, and you will experience the awesome and unmistakable power of victory over Satan and experience God's peace, which truly surpasses all understanding!

The Point Is

If we choose to hold onto negative relationships and allow negative thoughts to rule over our hearts, then we are keeping ourselves from possessing the biblical qualities found in Philippians 4:8: "Whatsoever things are true, whatsoever things are honest, whatsoever things are just, whatsoever things are pure, whatsoever things are lovely, whatsoever things are of good report; if there be any virtue, and if there be any praise, think on these things." Our goal as Christians should be to press on toward the great prize of peace that God has waiting for us when the reconstruction of our heart is complete. If we choose to allow these positive thoughts to rule our hearts, the God of peace will be in us always.

The following exercises have been designed to help you recognize the areas of your heart that Satan has damaged. If you truthfully evaluate your heart for the next seven days, God will be faithful to help you reconstruct it. However, if you need more time, *take it.* It is extremely important for you to find complete healing. There are no time restraints upon you. I encourage you to complete these exercises, because once you have, with God's help, reconstructed your heart, the reward will be tremendous. "And the peace of God, which passeth all understanding, shall keep your hearts and minds through Christ Jesus" (Philippians 4:7).

Now that you are ready to begin reconstructing your heart to find the prize of peace, put on your spiritual tool belt and grow spiritually through the following exercises:

These exercises will teach you how to:

- Replace anger with biblical qualities

- Appropriately respond to others

- Control your thoughts

Remember to put on your armor and give God control of your thoughts daily.

Fill in the appropriate answers as required per the instructions at the bottom of each exercise.

Biblical qualities to replace anger							
Quality	Sunday	Monday	Tuesday	Wednesday	Thursday	Friday	Saturday
Compassion							
Kindness							
Humility							
Gentleness							
Patience							
Forbearance							
Forgiveness							
Love							

Chart 1

1. At the end of each day, put a check mark beside the qualities that you demonstrated toward others.

2. Identify the areas that are not checked and ask God to help you develop those qualities.

3. Remember, your heart is under construction, so strive to rebuild your heart to be like Jesus.

Responding to others appropriately	S	M	TU	W	TR	F	S
Was I in harmony with him/her?							
Was I sympathetic?							
Was I compassionate?							
Did I demonstrate humility?							
Did I guard my tongue from returning evil?							
Did I turn from responding with evil?							
Did I seek and pursue peace?							
Did I respond in a gentle way?							
Did I show respect?							

Chart 2

1. On a scale of 1 to 10 (10 being the most consistent), define how consistently you demonstrate each of the above to your spouse, significant other, family, friends, co-workers, casual acquaintances, and even strangers. Write the number in the box for each day of the week.

2. Evaluate each area of weakness and resolve the specific problems through prayer.

3. Remember, your heart is under construction, so strive to rebuild your heart to be like Jesus.

Controlling your thoughts	S	M	T	W	T	F	S
True-Are my thoughts correct and true?							
Honest-Are my thoughts honorable to God & others?							
Just-Are my thoughts right? Will my thoughts lead me to right conduct?							
Pure-Are my thoughts Holy, separate from sin?							
Lovely-Do my thoughts lead me to develop a greater love for others?							
Good Report-Do my thoughts build the reputation of myself & others?							
Virtuous-Do my thoughts build moral / spiritual character in me?							
Praise worthy-Do my thoughts build up others?							
Respect-Do my thoughts build respect for myself and others?							

Chart 3

1. Keep a record of your thought patterns. Write *y* or *n* in answer to each question.

2. Evaluate each area of weakness and resolve the specific problems through prayer.

3. Remember, your heart is under construction, so strive to rebuild your heart to be like Jesus.

At the end of these spiritual exercises, when you have completed assessing the condition of your heart, think about the areas that need to change and share with God how you will change them.

Dear God, these are the areas of my heart that I need to change:

_____

_____

_____

_____

_____

_____

_____

_____

Dear God, this is how I will change my heart to be more like yours:

_____

_____

_____

_____

_____

_____

_____

_____

_____

Good Grief

In order to find complete healing through Christ, we *must* shape our hearts daily, put on our armor, and trust in God. We must also grieve the losses we suffered during our abuse and allow God to cleanse and restore us. With that thought in mind, during the reconstruction of your heart, were you surprised at your behavior pattern, especially where negativity was concerned? It is not uncommon to be negative after suffering abuse, and negativity is one of Satan's greatest tools. You can overcome your negativity by focusing on the positive changes taking place in your life as you continue the reconstruction of your heart.

To complete the reconstruction of our hearts, we need to grieve the damaged and hurt areas. Grief is typically identified with sadness, and it comes at different points in our lives. Contrary to popular thinking, grief is not always a bad thing because it brings closure to difficult situations and hurts.

To grieve is to heal and to grieve is to gain. Grieving allows us to come to terms with our losses and regain control of our lives. The stages of grief associated with abuse are a little different than the grieving stages we go through when we lose someone we love to death. However, there are some feelings that overlap because it is a loss nonetheless, whether or not mental, emotional, and/or physical abuse occurred. Grieving is vital in the healing process, but we tend to avoid it because there has not been an actual physical death. It is important for us to understand that parts of us have died, and those losses deserve to be grieved.

Some losses from abuse can never be restored, like one's virginity. This is a physical loss that provokes both mental and emotional pain. For example, saving oneself for the right man/woman and experiencing the natural longing for your wedding night can never be experienced. Your innocence was stolen from you without your permission. Now you have to deal with the past pain as well as confront the current pain associated with the previous loss. This is an ongoing abuse. The act that created the loss is over, but the devastation continues.

Often, inner conflict is created by horrible experiences from our past. We cannot seem to get the bad experiences out of our thoughts. These thoughts are thrown at us by our mind monsters. They hide themselves strategically along the road of our lives, and then as we unsuspectingly travel through our present daily life, they jump out and frighten us when we are most vulnerable. Once we are able to recognize our losses and grieve them, it allows us to conquer and maintain control over the mind monsters and move on with our lives without their interference.

We may feel that we are not strong enough to deal with the grieving process, and this is true where the flesh is concerned. However, Philippians 4:13 reassures us that we "can do all things through Christ which strengtheneth" us. With that knowledge, we should boldly take God's hand and grieve the hurt and losses in our heart as we continue our healing journey.

In 1969, Elisabeth Kubler-Ross originally defined the five stages of grief in her book *On Death and Dying*. Her five stages of grief include denial, anger, bargaining, depression, and acceptance. I personally discovered that I needed to conquer six stages of grief that were directly related to my abuse.

I have defined my personal six stages of grief as denial, blame, bargaining, anger, acceptance, and forgiveness. I learned through my own experience that this is the order of grieving for one who has been abused. We must start at the beginning and work our way to the end because one stage builds upon the other. Through each stage, as I surrendered myself and my pain to God, I grew stronger! My strength and courage came from the Lord, and with *his* help I was able to complete my healing. I know you can complete your healing also. That is what this journey is about. *Always* get in your safe zone, put on your armor, trust God, and grieve your losses one stage at a time. Remember what you learned about Satan and *do not* allow him to sabotage your healing journey with his lies and deceit.

We will start at the beginning and work through the first five stages in this chapter. Stage six, which is forgiveness, will have its own chapter. It is *vital* for you to complete all six stages of healing. Do not rush yourself, and please allow enough time to complete each stage of healing before moving to the next. This is for *you!*

Each stage will begin with a scripture reference and a series of questions. The scripture references are to encourage you, give you strength, and grow you spiritually through the knowledge of God's Holy Word. The questions are designed to help you understand the feelings and emotions associated with each stage of grief and help you identify the areas that you need to grieve.

Stage One: Denial

"If we suffer, we shall also reign with Him: If we deny him, he also will deny us" (2 Timothy 2:12).

Get in your safe zone, put on your armor, and ask God to show you the truth by answering the following questions with yes, no, or short sentences where required:

1. Do you currently have disorganized thoughts? *Yes   or   No*   If no, have you experienced them in the past? *Yes   or   No*

2. Are you often emotionally unaffected by events that happen in your life? *Yes   or   No*

3. Have you ever contemplated suicide? *Yes   or   No*   If yes, when?

   _____

   _____

   _____

   _____

   _____

4. Do you still contemplate suicide? *Yes   or   No* If yes, have you talked with anyone about your feelings? *Yes   or   No*

5. Do you ever feel numb all over? *Yes   or   No*

6. Do you ever get hysterical? *Yes   or   No*

7. Do you experience feelings of euphoria? *Yes   or   No*

8. Do you ever feel like you are outside your body? *Yes or No*

9. Are you overly talkative? *Yes   or   No*

10. Do you have hyper behavior? *Yes   or   No*

11. Are you simply passive and never voice an opinion? *Yes   or   No*

Although we have already accepted Jesus as our Lord and Savior, Timothy 2:12 tells us "if we deny Him, He also will deny us." This includes not trusting him for our healing. He has no choice but to deny us the joy and unspeakable peace we are seeking if we do not trust him and follow his commands. The first stage in our healing is to acknowledge the sins that were committed against us and stop secretly hiding them in our hearts.

It is extremely difficult to acknowledge the vile sins that Satan cast upon us through our abuser(s). Personally, it was very difficult for me to acknowledge that my boss violently raped me when I was sixteen years old and stole my virginity. But in order to heal, I had to acknowledge that the man responsible for this unspeakable act of sin against my person was a pawn of Satan. Once I stopped denying the rape, I was able to grieve it to God!

Denial is simply defined by Webster as "a refusal to acknowledge." It is the first step we go through when grieving our abuse. This is the incubation period for the mind monsters. We refuse to believe what happened to us, so we act as if it never did by going through the normal motions of everyday life. We *act* as if everything is all right, reassuring others we are fine even when our behavior depicts otherwise. This is the way our minds try to buffer the emotional, mental, and/or physical abuse we have suffered. Below are the symptoms I suffered and behavior patterns I associated with during my period of denial:

1. Disorganized thoughts

2. Feeling unaffected

3. Suicidal thoughts

4. Feeling numb

5. Feeling euphoric or hysterical

6. Feeling outside the body

7. Alternating between overly talkative and extremely quiet

8. Hyperactive or passive-submissive behavior

Maybe you recognize some of the symptoms of denial. Perhaps you have had them in the past or are currently experiencing some of them. Circle the number beside the ones you identify with.

Now that you understand what denial is and how it affects your life, you need to release your denial and acknowledge to God the sin(s) that was committed against you and grieve it with him. Just speak it out loud, and if you need to, *cry!* God is with you, and he is protecting you. It is time to let go of the secret you carry. It is not really your exclusive secret because God already knows, and he is just waiting for you to share it with him openly. It hurts to remember these things, but you must refuse to let Satan control your life. Cry out to God in your pain. Just cry to Jesus! Ask him to restore you to the person he ultimately created you to be! Allow yourself to grieve your loss, be it physical, mental, emotional, or all of them put together. *Give it to God!* He is big enough to carry your burden for you. Acknowledge, cleanse, and purge! God is grieving with you, and he desires to free you from your pain. *This is good grieving!* Release it all to him, and when you are ready, continue your personal journey of courage and healing. Please do not allow Satan to hinder you or keep you hostage in the desert of denial. The last thing he wants is for you to find complete healing through Christ.

Write down what happened to you and what you are feeling now. Express and release your pain to God. Write as much as you need to for as long as you need to. Writing is a great way to purge, and you can address it directly to God. You do not have to share this with anyone else. It is exclusively between you and God, the merciful Lord of healing.

Dear God, I cannot deny the sins that were committed against me any longer. I acknowledge the evil, I grieve my losses, and I give my burdens to you now.

_____

_____

_____

_____

_____

_____

_____

_____

_____

_____

_____

_____

_____

_____

_____

_____

_____

_____

Stage Two: Blame

"And the man said, The woman whom thou gavest to be with me, she gave me of the tree, and I did eat. And the Lord God said unto the woman, What is this that thou hast done? And the woman said, The serpent beguiled me, and I did eat" (Genesis 3:12–13).

Get in your safe zone, put on your armor, and ask God to show you the truth by answering the following questions with yes, no, or short sentences where required:

1. Do you recreate different scenarios of the abuse in your mind? *Yes   or   No*   If yes, how often?

   _____

2. Do you get your feelings hurt easily?
Yes or No

3. Are you often emotionally hurt by those you feel are responsible for your abuse whether they are or not? *Yes or No*

4. Do you find yourself withdrawing from family, friends, work, God? *Yes or No*

5. Do you feel or think you deserved what happened to you? *Yes or No* If yes, why?

_____

6. Do you feel or think the abuse was your fault? *Yes or No* If no, whose fault was it?

_____

7. Do you have low self-esteem? *Yes or No*

8. Do you respect yourself and others?
Yes or No

9. Are you ready to place the blame where it belongs and give it to God? *Yes or No* If no, what or who is stopping you?

_____

Webster's definition of blame is "to place fault." The need to blame others began with Adam and Eve in the garden of Eden. It is a human reaction of the flesh to blame others or ourselves for unpleasant experiences in our lives, especially if abuse is the root cause of the bad experience. Oftentimes in abusive situations, the abused feels responsible for the abuser's transgressions against them, even if they had absolutely no control over the abuse. This is when the mind monsters learn to crawl and eventually walk. Our thoughts are consumed with reliving the abuse, and we run different scenarios in our mind, trying desperately to find answers to unexplained actions. Usually during this time of emotional and mental confusion, we alternate between blaming others and/or ourselves. The persons being blamed can range from close family members to casual acquaintances depending on the type of abuse suffered and how many different scenarios the mind monsters run through our thoughts. Below are some of the symptoms I suffered and behavior patterns I associated with during my period of blame:

1. Recreating different scenarios of the abuse in my mind

2. Hurt feelings toward those I felt were responsible, whether real or imagined

3. Distancing myself from others, withdrawing

4. Feeling that I deserved what happened

5. Constantly thinking that it was exclusively my fault

6. Low self-esteem

7. Loss of self-respect

8. Feelings of shame

Maybe you recognize some of the symptoms of blame. Perhaps you have had them in the past or are currently experiencing some of them now. Circle the number beside the ones you identify with.

It started in the garden of Eden, and it still happens today! Adam blamed Eve, and Eve blamed the serpent (who was Satan). Someone always has to be blamed for every bad event in our lives. The truth of the matter is we often blame ourselves even though we could not prevent what happened to us. We may have been too young, too scared, too confused, or too spiritually lost to recognize the sinful behavior in our environment. The shame and guilt of early childhood abuse has a way of altering the reality we live in. The abuse, whether sexual, physical, mental, or emotional, skews our ability to recognize what should be a normal family environment. Abuse from the cradle truly puts a slant on our ability to recognize the difference between right and wrong and good and evil.

So we grow up blaming ourselves for what they did to us! There is only one culprit that has earned the title of such deceit, and his name is Satan. He loves to take the young and tender heart and chain it in his dungeon of deceit. Why should we know better than to believe him and his lies? We do not know the difference until we are introduced to Jesus Christ. Then his light shines in the darkness, and we see how Satan deceived us, just as he deceived Eve. We had no control over our abuser(s)! They were, and perhaps still are, bound in Satan's chains of lust and violence. Nevertheless, we were the unfortunate ones in their path when they committed their horrible evil against us, and although we did not deserve it, we suffered or are still suffering because of it!

In our moment of anguish and despair, Satan, disguised as the great deceiver, swiftly moved in and chained us in his dungeon of deceit, whispering his lies in our ears. Perhaps he told you that you were damaged and no good to anyone. Perhaps he made you believe that you were worthless, nothing less than a despicable shell of human flesh. Perhaps he even made you believe that you were not deserving of true love and not worthy of a beautiful relationship. But he did not stop there; perhaps he told you if you told anyone, he or she would not believe you. Satan deceived you into believing that you were the one responsible for the abuse and convinced you that you brought it on yourself. It is hard to admit, but I listened to his lies and allowed myself to remain chained in his dungeon of deceit for twenty-four years!

The good news is, I am no longer in Satan's dungeon of deceit, and you do not have to be chained there either! We are children of God, and as God's children, we can see the truth. What happened to us was not our fault in any way.

It actually feels good to finally understand it was not my fault, and *it was not your fault.* There is only one who is ultimately responsible for what happened, and his name is Satan. However, we must understand that our abuser(s) made the choice to allow Satan to manipulate them. We can take comfort in knowing that they will stand in judgment before the great, white throne of God and be judged for their actions. Knowing this, it is time to stop playing the blame game and come to terms with who is at fault! Their sinful actions were not because of you!

Give your blame game to God. Speak out loud who really is to blame. If you were raped and you do not know their name(s), refer to them as Satan's pawn(s). You will be amazed how awesome it feels to peel off another layer of pain. God already knows who sinned against you, and he promises us in his Holy Word that he will deal with them for us. Put your trust in God and give your burden of guilt to him because it is not yours to carry anymore. Place your shame where it belongs, at the feet of Jesus, and let the healing continue. God is waiting for you to grieve it to him.

Take this time to *grieve it* and *leave it!* Allow yourself to *feel* and to *heal.* Call on Christ, and he will comfort you. This is good grieving! Write down the person(s) responsible for your anguish. This is for you and God only. You do not have to share this with anyone else unless you want to.

Dear God, I realize that the abuse was not my fault, and I will no longer blame myself for their evil actions. I clearly understand that Satan used the following people to torment me:

I _____ (your name) realize that I was not and am not responsible for the sinful acts that were committed against me.

I _____ (your name) also realize that _____ (your abuser(s) name(s)) was/were responsible for the devastation in my life due to their sinful and abusive actions against me.

I _____ (your name) understand God has helped me place the blame where it belongs and with his help I can move on with my grief and continue my healing.

"It Wasn't My Fault"

I didn't ask for it to happen, but it did.
I didn't want it to happen, but it did.
I tried to deny that it happened, but it did.
I tried not to blame myself, but I did.
God told me to stop blaming myself, so I did!

Stage Three: Bargaining

"Lying lips are abomination to the Lord: But they that deal truly are His delight" (Proverbs 12:22).

Get in your safe zone, put on your armor, and ask God to show you the truth by answering the following questions with yes, no, or short sentences where required:

1. Do you rationalize daily or routine activities? *Yes   or   No*

2. Do you feel you have to make deals to get things done for you? *Yes   or   No*
   If yes, why do you feel this way?

   _____

3. Are you able to accept favors or help from family and friends without feeling like you owe them something in return? *Yes   or   No*
   If no, what do you owe them?

   _____

4. Do you feel like you are worth the amount of love and friendship others try to give you? *Yes* or *No* If no, why not?

_____

5. Are you suffering from loss of self-worth? *Yes* or *No* If yes, what would it take for you to reclaim it?

_____

Webster defines bargaining as a contract; a gainful transaction. Bargaining occurs when you try to rationalize the abuse. The mind monster tries to get you to sell yourself short of God's glory, and your thoughts become obsessed with making a deal with someone, anyone, *even God!*

We try desperately to bargain our way out of having to accept what really happened. Our thoughts fluctuate between *yes, but, if only,* or *if I do this, will you do*... Whatever the mind monster tells us will make it better. But in reality, we can not make a gainful transaction with a mind monster. Ultimately, we lose! However, we can make a gainful transaction with God. We should not sell our soul to the devil when we can redeem it for peace and joy! God does not desire to make a deal with us; his desire is for us to find healing through him. He can squash the mind monster and set us free from its evil grip. When we realize God is the only one that should be in control of our thoughts, the need to bargain dissipates.

Below are some of the behavioral patterns I experienced and thought processes that I associated with during my period of bargaining:

1. Rationalizing routine activities like going to nightclubs and excessive drinking

2. Unable to accept help or favors unless I could give something in return

3. Loss of self-worth

4. Fluctuating between promiscuous and prudish behavior

Maybe you recognize some of the symptoms of bargaining. Perhaps you have had them in the past or are currently experiencing some of them. Circle the number beside the ones you identify with.

What better transaction can we make than to exchange our pain for God's peace? Why would we want to deal with Satan when all he has to offer us are more deceitful lies? There is absolutely nothing to gain trying to deal with Satan. However, we have everything to gain with God. All he wants is for us to deal truthfully with him. He already knows the truth;

he just wants us to show him that we too know the truth.

When we share our secrets with God and give him our baggage by praying the truths of our heart to him, he delights in us. Looking back over my life, I can see how I tried to bargain my way out of accepting what happened. I tried desperately to rationalize the attack. I allowed Satan to alter my life by refusing to see the reality associated with the abuse, and I lost twenty-four precious years of my life chained in the dungeon of deceit. Praise God for his love, mercy, and grace because he did not leave me there to rot! He was waiting for me to come to him, and now that I have, I cannot imagine my life without him. There are no more bargaining days ahead for me; God and the truth have set me free.

You can be set free also. Take this time and deal truthfully with God; surrender another layer of your pain and be healed. Do not be afraid to make one of the most gainful transactions of your life by exchanging your baggage for his healing touch. Stop bargaining with Satan! Humbly bow down before God and make your transaction through prayer and supplication. Leave your bargains and burdens at the foot of the cross and arise, healed from bargaining in the name of Jesus.

Get in your safe zone, put on your armor, and ask God to show you the truth and exchange your bargaining bag-

gage for God's healing touch through prayer because prayer works!

Prayer time—there is no time limit; pray as long as you need to and release all your burdens to God and be *healed* through the awesome power of *prayer* in the name of Jesus Christ.

Stage Four: Anger

"Dearly beloved, avenge not yourselves, but rather give place unto wrath: for it is written, Vengeance is mine; I will repay, saith the Lord" (Romans 12:19).

"Therefore, as I live, saith the Lord God, I will even do according to thine anger, and according to thine envy which thou hast used out of thy hatred against them; and I will make myself known among them, when I have judged thee" (Ezekiel 35:11).

Get in your safe zone, put on your armor, and ask God to show you the truth by answering the following questions with yes, no, or short sentences where required:

Inward Anger

1. Do you feel guilty about everything whether you should or not? *Yes   or   No*   If yes, why?

2. Do you often experience quiet or dark moods? *Yes or No* If yes, how often? _____ When was the last one? _____

3. Do your family or friends notice or comment about your moods? *Yes or No*

4. Are you antisocial? *Yes or No* If yes, when was the last time you went out or to a function?

   _____

5. Do you experience depression on a regular basis? *Yes or No* If yes, when was your last bout of depression? _____

6. Do you take medication for your depression? *Yes or No* If yes, do you feel like it is working for you? *Yes or No* If no, have you contacted your doctor about it? *Yes or No–* If no, will you contact your doctor soon? *Yes or No* If no, why not?

   _____

7. Do you suffer from lack of self-worth? *Yes or No*

8. Do you understand God gave his only Son for you? *Yes or No*

9. Do you understand God thought you were worth it? *Yes or No* If no, who did Christ die for? (Circle all that apply)
   Select people   A few sinners   Me

10. Do you suffer from lack of self-respect?
    Yes   or   No   If yes, how can you get it back?

    _____

Outward Anger

1. Is your temper easily provoked? *Yes   or   No*

2. Do you feel mad longer than you should?
   Yes   or   No

3. How long do you typically stay mad at someone?

   _____

   _____

   _____

4. Do you have fits of uncontrollable rage?
   Yes   or   No If yes, how do you feel when the rage is over? _____.
   Was it worth it? *Yes   or   No*

5. Are you confrontational? *Yes or No*
   If yes, why?

   _____

6. Can you accept constructive criticism?
   Yes or No If no, why not?

   _____

7. Do you instigate or provoke arguments?
   Yes or No If yes, why?_____
   Are you quick to make a fist and feel the urge
   to physically hit someone? *Yes or No* If yes,
   how often do you react this way? (Circle one)
   Every time Sometimes

8. Have you actually hit someone before?
   Yes or No If yes, when was the last time?
   _____ Did you feel better or
   worse after you hit them? (Circle one)
   Better Worse

9. Do you believe in your heart God can take away
   your anger? *Yes or No* If no, why not?

   _____

10. Are you ready to exchange your anger for God's
    healing? *Yes or No* If no, why not?

    _____

Webster defines anger as "a violent passion; excited by real or supposed injury; resentment: to irritate." According to Ezekiel 35:11, God makes it abundantly clear he will judge us based on how we handled our anger toward others. Even though we did not deserve the sins committed against us, we must not return evil for evil. This is the strongest force the mind monster uses against us. Feelings of anger typically provoke the thoughts of *Why me?* or *How dare you!* These thoughts trigger our emotions, and we begin to feel resentment because of the damages created in our heart from the abuse. We sense the unfairness and often feel abandoned and/or powerless. Then we deal with our anger by turning it *inward or outward.*

Anger is a very powerful *emotion.* Some people use it to gain control of others through manipulation and fear. Some people cannot control it, and some simply suppress it. No matter how anger is used, it is unproductive and destructive. Anger can alternate between inward and outward. After my initial abuse, I had an uncontrollable outward anger. My family, friends, and co-workers did not understand my temperamental attitude because I had never told anyone about the rape. It festered inside of me and became the root of my hairtrigger temper. After several years of outward anger and many requests for me to learn to control my anger issues, I turned it inward. I went from rage to submissive! Neither of these was healthy, and I suffered the symptoms of my deep anger in the following ways:

Inward anger:

1. Feelings of excessive guilt

2. Quiet, dark moods

3. Antisocial

4. Depression

5. Lack of self-worth

6. Lack of self-respect

7. Submissive behavior

Outward anger:

1. Quick tempered

2. Feeling mad for longer than normal

3. Uncontrollable fits of rage

4. Confrontational

5. Unable to accept constructive criticism

6. Arrogant and unruly

Maybe you recognize some of the symptoms of anger. Perhaps you have had them in the past or are currently experiencing some of them now. Circle the numbers that best describe how you handled your anger in the past and how you handle your anger now. At the end of each one, write the letter *p, n,* or *b* to designate *past, now,* or *both.*

Struggling with our anger is not what God intended for our life. He created us for a greater purpose, and when we allow anger to destroy our bodies and our minds, we are destroying our earthly temple. God gave us our body to be used for his glory. When we allow evil to take up residence inside of us in the form of anger, we might as well be saying to God, *I refuse to give you your glory!* As hard as it may be, we must give our anger to God and let him be in control for us. The first time you master giving God your anger, you will be amazed how awesome the end result is. Remember, there is no situation too big for him to handle.

When we turn our anger *inward,* we end up hurting ourselves in multiple ways. By turning the anger inward, we magnify the guilt we already feel. We generally feel guilt when we feel we have violated our own standards or we feel we have let someone we love down. Turning anger inward typically results in deep depression and isolation. When we suppress anger, we open ourselves to even more negative feelings and emotions, which ultimately can result in physical conditions brought on by the inner stress. When you are struggling with inward anger, pray and/or write to God, asking him to help you control your inward anger by releasing Satan's hold on you.

When we turn our anger *outward*, it is very obvious to the people around us. We, the abused victims, demonstrate hostility or aggression to those we feel are responsible for our abuse, whether they are or not. Often, the ability to control our temper is lost, and the smallest incidents, whether real or imagined, will insight our rage. This rage, at times, can be uncontrollable. When we calm down, we typically feel remorseful for our actions, and we may even apologize.

Often, in outward rage, the mind monster convinces us the person on the receiving end of our rage is deserving of our actions. This is not always the case because we tend to direct our anger toward those who are closest to us. Our outburst often leaves the person on the receiving end wondering what he or she did wrong. In this situation, the outward anger is hard on the recipient and the victim. In some situations, the rage is directed at the one responsible for the abuse. This hostility, although deserved, is not the best action for us to take. Some abusers thrive on the negative attention, and it could incite further abuse. Besides, God tells us not to return evil for evil. The next time you find yourself in a confrontational situation, cast Satan behind you in the name of Jesus and simply turn and walk away. Start praising God with every step, and he will give you the strength and courage you need to keep walking! Arguing never resolves anything!

Unfortunately, we cannot change our past, but God can help us change our future. Take a few moments to think about how you have been handling your anger and how you are going to handle it from this point forward. You have the authority as a child of God to cast Satan behind you in the name of Jesus and walk away from confrontations. It will not be easy to change your anger patterns, but Philippians 4:13 reminds us that we "can do all things through Christ which strengtheneth" us. Lose another layer of pain by grieving your anger to God and allow him to help you control it. Write down how you cope with your inward anger; then write down the hot buttons that trigger your outward rage.

This is how I cope with my inward anger:

_____

_____

_____

_____

_____

These are the hot buttons that provoke my outward anger:

_____

_____

_____

_____

_____

This is how I will give God control over my anger starting now:

_____

_____

_____

_____

_____

Stage Five: Acceptance

"Let the words of my mouth, and the meditation of my heart, be acceptable in thy sight, O LORD, my strength, and my redeemer" (Psalm 19:14).

Get in your safe zone, put on your armor, and ask God to show you the truth by answering the following questions with yes, no, or short sentences where required:

1. Have you been able to recall your abuse without too many emotional side effects? *Yes or No* If no, who can help you see the truth about your abuse?

   _____

2. Have you realized you had no control over your abuser(s) and their sinful actions were not your fault? *Yes or No* If no, who can help you realize this?

   _____

3. Have you been able to talk with others about your abuse? *Yes or No*

4. Are you able to accept help or favors from others without feeling guilt or having to do something for them in return? *Yes or No* If no, who wants you to exchange your baggage for his healing?

   _____

5. Do you have the ability to remain calm in confrontational situations and take the appropriate actions to resolve the conflict even if it means

walking away? *Yes   or   No*   If no, who can help you change how you react to confrontational situations?

_____

6. Have you realized you are a person of worth? *Yes   or   No*

7. Have you found your self-respect? *Yes   or   No*

8. If you answered *no* to either of the last two questions, how can you reclaim these losses?

_____

_____

_____

Acceptance is defined by Webster as "a bill of exchange accepted." When we reach acceptance, our battle is nearing completion, but we have not won the war yet. Acceptance happens when we finally come to terms with the abuse and what we have lost. This is where the grieving process begins to reveal the healing. The denial has passed. The blame has been placed. The bargain (transaction) has been made. The anger has been released. The acceptance has finally hit home. Here is where the rubber meets the road; we face our abuse with a sad sense of calmness, a kind of resignation that allows us to accept what happened.

Our acceptance does not mean that we will forget what happened to us, who did it, or how long it lasted. Neither does it mean that we will never feel the element of our abuse again or forget the nature by which the abuse and ensuing losses came into being. It simply means we have acknowledged the abuse happened, and we finally understand it was not our fault.

To me, my abuse is like a bad scar upon my flesh, a burn scar. I am able to look at it, and I remember how it got there, I remember how bad it hurt when it happened, but when I touch it, it does not hurt me *anymore*. There is a peace that comes with acceptance. God's peace! He delivers his grace and mercy to your aching soul. Endless days of torment, pain, anguish, and agony fade into the distance as his holy light penetrates the darkness.

This loss of darkness allows your days to become brighter; the mind monsters lose control over your thoughts. You begin to recognize the mind monster's tactics, and in doing so, you are able to overcome Satan's evil whisperings in your mind. When he throws painful memories your way, you are able to say, "Get thee behind me, Satan, in the name of Jesus because you have no reign over me anymore." Each time you dismiss the mind monster, the bad thoughts grow farther apart and you become stronger, especially if you are putting on your armor and submitting to God by giving him your thoughts *daily*. Below are the traits I have achieved because of my acceptance:

1. I can recall or think about the abuse without extreme emotional side effects

2. I realize that it was not my fault

3. I can now accept help or favors from others and simply say *thank you*

4. I am calm

5. I am able to think before reacting to a situation and take the appropriate action(s)

6. My self-worth is restored

7. My self-respect is restored

8. I can talk with others about my abuse

9. I desire to share my testimony of how *God healed me*

Maybe you recognize some of the traits of acceptance. Perhaps you are currently experiencing some of them. Circle the numbers that best describe how you feel at this point of your healing.

Once we have accepted our past, we are able to learn from it and grow spiritually through Christ. We should view each day as a new day in Christ! Every obstacle Satan sets in our path can be overcome as we grow stronger through each stage of our healing. Loosening Satan's grasp on our life allows us to see with spiritual eyes and hear with spiritual ears.

We cannot speak words of truth about our life unless we have taken the time to meditate in our hearts the events that have led us to who we have become in Christ. Speaking for myself, I have finally accepted my unpleasant past. I have examined it thoroughly and, at times, thought I would die a physical death because of the pain that racked my inner being. At other times, I could not breathe; the tears that fell from my eyes were being torn from my tormented soul because of someone else's sin. The tattered ravages of his lust left deep scars, the kind that go beyond the flesh, all the way to the core of who I was. How horrible was my fake existence. The denial! The blame! The bargaining! The anger! Then finally the acceptance!

But I cannot take the glory for where I am today. That praise belongs exclusively to God. He has graciously granted me the strength and courage through his son Jesus Christ to actually accept what happened to me and not only move beyond it but to share his great love and healing with others that have suffered abuse. I know the positive change he brought to my life, and I know he wants to do the same for all who have suffered at Satan's wicked hand. Even though my life has not been as I would have dreamed it, my hope is renewed and my restoration continues.

If you are struggling with acceptance, take this time and pray to God, asking him to help you *accept* your past and *change* your future. *Grieve* your losses to him openly and without shame because he knows the tattered ravages of your soul and the deep scars upon your heart. Grieve it to God!

It is not an everyday event to realize that it is okay to accept your past. But I am thankful today is your day! Complete your acceptance by acknowledging the following:

I _____ (your name), accept the sins committed against me by _____ (your abuser(s) name), and from this moment forward I release Satan's chains of bondage from my heart, mind, body, soul, and spirit into the mighty healing hands of Jesus Christ.

Stage six of the grieving process is forgiveness, and the next chapter is devoted to it. *Forgiveness* is vital because it *completes the healing process.* If you think you are unable to forgive, think again! Jesus forgave us as he hung on the cross at Calvary. He said with outstretched arms nailed to a wooden cross, "Father, forgive them for they know not what they do" (Luke 23:24). He said this after he had been scourged beyond recognition. Knowing this, can you still say you are unable to forgive?

Be reassured that you can master forgiveness with the help of Jesus Christ. Open your heart and your mind to the greatest relief you will ever feel as you *complete* your personal journey of healing.

Faithful Forgiveness

Forgiveness is the key that unlocks your heart's door to *peace!* We cannot pick and choose the stages of healing that we think we can handle; rather, we *must* surrender our hearts and baggage to God through each stage. Otherwise, we are allowing Satan to cheat us out of our complete healing.

If I could stand in your shoes now and do this for you, I would. But I cannot. Only you, through Christ, can do this. I personally assure you, you can and will be able to forgive if you allow yourself to stop thinking in the flesh and submit yourself before God. He will take your hand and lead you through it. He knows you will never forget, but he also knows you will never find the peace you are searching for if you do not have the courage to complete this journey of healing. Without taking the final step in the healing process you are denying yourself everything you have come this far for *complete healing through Christ.* It is time for you to come out of the desert, find your oasis, and drink from the fountain of Living Water!

Stage Six: Forgiveness

"And when ye stand praying, forgive, if ye have ought against any: that your Father also which is in heaven may forgive you your trespasses. But if ye do not forgive, neither will your Father which is in heaven forgive your trespasses" (Mark 11:25–26).

Get in your safe zone, put on your armor, and ask God to show you the truth by answering the following questions with yes, no, or short sentences where required:

1. Do you understand forgiveness is a necessity? *Yes or No* If no, who can help you realize the importance of forgiveness?

   _____

2. Do you understand without forgiveness God can not complete your healing? *Yes or No* If no, who can help you find complete healing through forgiveness?

   _____

3. Are you ready with God's help to forgive your abuser(s)? *Yes   or   No*   If no, what will it take for you to forgive?

_____

_____

_____

_____

_____

Forgiveness is defined by Webster as "the act of forgiving; to forgive: Forgive: to cease to feel resentment against (an offender)." For many, forgiveness is the hardest stage of grief. We may have reached acceptance, but we feel forgiveness is not an option. Unfortunately, if we refuse to forgive those who have sinned against us, we deprive ourselves of complete healing.

If we do not forgive our abuser(s), we bind ourselves to them. These are the unholy chains of bondage that Satan wraps tightly around us. Therefore, as hard as it may be, we *must* come to terms with forgiving our abuser(s). One way to view it is forgiveness is not a choice; it is a requirement! Not only is it a requirement, it is God's law. Mark 11:25–26 puts forgiveness in biblical perspective. The scripture clearly states if we are unable to forgive those that have trespassed against us, God will not forgive us our trespasses. When we stand in judgment, God will not forgive us if we have not forgiven. These scriptures do not define forgiveness as a choice, but rather a judgment day requirement!

For some of us, even knowing in our hearts our eternity is affected by forgiveness, we still feel we cannot forgive. We continue to hold fast to the heavy burdens we carry, allowing Satan to beat us down and break our spirit day after day. But we must remember, for our hearts to be like Jesus, we must forgive.

As Christ hung on the cross he said, "Father, forgive them; for they know not what they do" (Luke 23:24). If Jesus was able to forgive those that scourged him and nailed his hands and feet to a wooden cross, who are we to be greater than Christ and not forgive? Jesus knew the beauty of forgiveness, so why do we hinder and hurt ourselves? The Bible tells us in Luke 6:37, "Judge not, and ye shall not be judged: Condemn not, and ye shall not be condemned: Forgive, and ye shall be forgiven:" This passage clearly teaches us we are not to judge or condemn but to forgive so that we may also be forgiven.

Forgiveness is truly a beautiful way to find God's ultimate *peace* and live life refreshed and anew each day through Christ. In order to have this peace, we must forgive our transgressors their trespasses against us. Because God is a just God, if we choose not to forgive, neither will our Father in heaven forgive us. Please think about what this scripture is actually saying to us. God is specifically instructing us to forgive anyone we have something against.

Satan knows how hard it is for us to forgive those who have contributed to the misery in our lives, and he uses it to keep us bound in his dungeon of deceit. Webster's definition of the word *anyone* is defined as "any person." It is not defined as any person *except* those who have done terrible things to you. Nor is it defined as any person *other than* those you choose to refuse to forgive. Simply put, anyone is *any person* regardless of gender, religious background, color, origin of birth, and sinful nature.

It is a good thing Christ did not have such particular standards when he was hanging on the cross at Calvary, shedding his blood to cover our sins—not just my sins, but your sins and our transgressors sins also! Who are we to put ourselves higher than Christ and say we are not capable of forgiving? We have been forgiven, and the price Christ paid was far greater than you or I will ever have to pay. Just something for you to think about as you ponder your position on forgiveness.

I would like to share part of my testimony with you. When I was struggling so hard with forgiveness, I turned to God's Holy Word to help me understand not only why it was so important for me to forgive but also why my eternal life resulted in the need to forgive. God helped me to understand the beauty of forgiveness and the freedom it brings to your soul, mind, and spirit. I realized the only true way to forgiveness was to have a heart like Jesus and to do exactly what he did: forgive my transgressor's sins against me just as Jesus forgave my sins against him.

You see, as Christ hung on the cross, in his last moments of agony, he felt the sins of the world, including mine, yours, and our transgressors', wash over him. In that moment, he was separated from God, our Father; he felt everything we feel now. But that did not stop him from crying out, "Father, forgive them; for they know not what they do" (Luke 23:24).

Many times, I have reflected about the rape inflicted on me and the way it altered my life so dramatically. I wondered to myself if my transgressor had of known the impact he was having on my life, would he have committed such a horrible act of sin against me? I cannot fathom what happened in his life that brought him to a place of such desolate sin. I will never know his personal history. It could have been one of abuse and someone else's sin forced upon him as a little boy. It could have been the rejection of God as his Lord and Savior. I realize it does not excuse him from his actions or the pain and suffering he caused in my life, but it allows me to understand why the Bible tells us in Matthew 18:7 "offenses must come." Those offenses are from our one true enemy—Satan.

I must admit: I held great hatred in my heart toward my abuser for many years, totally unwilling to forgive him of the sins he committed against me. I remained steadfast in the course of my own self-destruction. I dwelt in utter darkness, nurturing the bitter seeds of depression. I denied myself the joys of life, withholding the pleasures of true love from my heart, allowing myself to be devoured second by second, minute by minute, day by day, and eventually year by year with hopelessness and desperation. The functioning shell of my person performed routine daily tasks, and at brief moments I glimpsed thoughts of normalcy and treasured brief moments of happiness. Bust mostly I dwelt in the vast wasteland of unforgiveness.

I dwelt in this unhappy state for twenty-four years! Even though I chose not to forgive, God was still watching over me. He wept every time I wept. He relived my pain with me time and again. I can look back and see the times he beckoned me to find healing through him, but I refused. He was waiting for me to come to him and give him my burdens. I alone chose not to.

Then one day in the ultimate pit of my desperate despair, I finally looked *up!* There was nowhere else left for me to go. Satan had me so tightly bound I could not move, much less breathe. On my knees, alone in my bedroom with my head down in my hands, I wept! In my despair, I finally cried out, "God, help me!" In an instant, he touched me! And the joy that filled my soul was not of this earth because when he touched me, he made me whole! My tears of pain and anguish turned to tears of joy and renewed hope. I still cried, but not for the same reasons as before, I said out loud for my ears and God to hear, "I forgive him, Lord. I forgive him!"

I wish there were words to describe the experience, but nothing this side of heaven can compare. My life forever changed that day, and God has taken the years of my abuse and ensuing bad choices and turned them into a blessing. Had he not been with me through my tormented years and faithful to hear my plea of help and heal me, I would not have been able to write this book for you with the Holy Spirit as my guide.

So you see, I know firsthand how hard it is to forgive, but I also know firsthand how beautiful the act of forgiveness is and the blessings that are in store for those who will surrender all to God.

Please do not miss this beautiful opportunity of complete healing. Do not let Satan persuade you to surrender to his lies. The last thing he wants you to do is forgive. That is his final hold on you. I assure you, you will be amazed as you physically feel the weight lift. I have forgiven my abuser, and I have also forgiven myself. I will not trade where I am now for the world or Satan's bondage ever again!

That is why I would stand in your shoes for you if I could. I personally know where you are and how you feel right now. But I also know where you can be and how you can feel when you truly surrender your heart, just as Christ did, to *forgiveness*. Once you give it over to God, you will wonder why you were obstinate for so long. But do not beat yourself up over it; just bask in the healing glory of the Lord and begin every day anew with hope and keep on forgiving your transgressor(s) for the rest of your earthly life.

Take this wonderful opportunity set before you on your healing journey to bow down before God on your knees and surrender your pain and anguish to him through the beautiful act of prayerful forgiveness. Exchange the bitter baggage in your heart for God's unspeakable peace. Release your heavy burden and cry out to God for his help. Declare out loud who you forgive; call them by name. If you do not know your abuser's name, then declare out loud that you forgive the one(s) that sinned mightily against you. Rest assured that God knows exactly who they are. Feel God's healing spirit embrace you! Feel the breathless joy that fills your soul! Feel the last chains of bondage fall from you, and bask in the beauty of complete healing through Jesus Christ. Let the Holy Spirit fill you with joy, hope, love, and peace. Let your tears of pain be turned into tears of relief and joy. When you have forgiven your abuser(s) and found God's peace, complete the following statement:

I _____
(Your Name) have forgiven the following person/people that have committed sinful acts against me.

_____

_____

_____

I am certain that God is well pleased with you for surrendering your heart to forgiveness! From this moment forward, you will be forever changed, provided you do not allow Satan to bind you again. There are daily battles that still have to be fought, but victory is yours, and you will remain victorious as long as you stay vigilant. The next chapter will help you understand how to maintain your freedom through Christ as you take a scriptural stroll down victory lane.

"I Didn't, But He Did"

I didn't want to; I didn't think I could.
I didn't want to, but I knew I should.
I didn't want to, but God said I would.
I didn't feel I could from the start.
I didn't feel I could change my heart.
I didn't feel I could find the courage.
I didn't feel, but God said I would.
I didn't reject his love.

I didn't reject his healing.
I didn't close my eyes.
I didn't cover my ears.
I didn't refuse to forgive.
I didn't change my heart, *but he did!*

Vigilant Victory

Once we have grieved our losses and come to the healing peace of forgiveness, we must be vigilant in our battle against Satan. His sole purpose is to seek us out and try to sway us through his lies and deceit to surrender to him, which causes us to stumble in our victory.

Satan's greatest glory comes when we fail to stay close to God and allow him to steal our joy. Once he has stolen our joy, the peace of God fades from our heart as we lose our spiritual eyes and ears. Once Satan has managed to harden our heart, he places scales upon our senses, and we are once again effectively chained in his dark dungeon of deceit to receive his torture. The mind monsters begin to attack; we fall away from family, friends, and church. We revisit our anger and relive our abuse. Doubt becomes our best friend as we move backward in time all the way to the beginning and find ourselves nursing the seeds of bitterness once again.

These seeds, so strategically and tragically sown by Satan, grow into a fresh crop of barren unhappiness. Does this sound familiar? It should because we have managed to return to the garden of evil. Like earthly crops, we too recycle our emotions based on the fertilizer being thrown on our hearts. Once the soil or heart has been depleted of its nutrients or emotions, no good fruit is produced. This is exactly where Satan wants to keep us. The only way back to God and his peace is to retrace our steps. We must reseek God's will in our lives through prayer and ask him to show us his truths again.

It is not unusual to go through the grieving process more than once, nor is it uncommon to reclaim the victim attitude, causing us to lose our feelings of forgiveness, the forgiveness we gave our transgressor(s) as well as the forgiveness we gave ourselves. Just remember these feelings are not true; they are the result of Satan's deceit and lies. The deceiver has deceived! The captor has taken us captive!

Micah 7:19 reminds us how merciful and compassionate God is. When we ask God for repentance, he is faithful to forgive us. He throws our sins into the depths of the sea. That is why the blood of Christ was shed at Calvary—so that we may be forgiven of our sins. God never throws our sins back in our face. However, Satan would have us believe otherwise. That is why it is so important to learn God's Holy Word and stay close to him in your spiritual walk. The more you learn about God and his ways, the less likely you are to listen to Satan and his lies. The more you know about God, the more power you have over Satan.

Victory is ours through Jesus Christ, and God's unspeakable peace is ours through our vigilance. To maintain our victory over Satan, we must learn how to be effective warriors and keep ourselves free of his chains by remaining steadfast in our Christian walk. It is up to us read, learn, and apply the things God is going to revel to us as we put on the shoes of the gospel and take a scriptural stroll down victory lane.

Scripture One: 1 Corinthians 15:57

"But thanks be to God, which giveth us the victory through our Lord Jesus Christ."

God is reaffirming that our victory over Satan comes through our Lord and Savior Jesus Christ. Satan has no authority over us once we accept Christ. It is imperative that we understand we cannot do anything in our own human strength, but we can do all things through Christ who strengthens us, provided we have submitted ourselves to God. So, when Satan tries to come at you, all you have to do is claim your victory by casting Satan behind you in the name of Jesus Christ. This sends him back where he belongs because Satan has no choice but to flee at the victorious name of Jesus Christ. It is like scalding him with hot water!

Scripture Two: 1 Peter 5:8

> "Be sober, Be vigilant; because your adversary the devil, as a roaring lion, walketh about, seeking whom he may devour."

God is reminding us how Satan walks about seeking, waiting for a chance to devour us. That is why we must "be sober" and "be vigilant." We have to keep our spiritual eyes and ears open all the time because we are daily targets for Satan's darts of deception. This is why it is so important for us to put on our armor and submit ourselves to God every morning. We must daily prepare ourselves for battle.

Scripture Three: Job 10:15–17

> "I am full of confusion; therefore see thou mine affliction; for it increaseath. Thou huntest me as a fierce lion: and again thou shewest thyself marvelous upon me."

God is revealing to us how Job felt about Satan's attack on his life. Job realized his only adversary was Satan, and he also understood how Satan causes confusion in our minds. If we allow him, Satan inflicts mental, emotional, and physical pain upon us. Job also clearly understood that Satan seeks us out. He literally walks about "seeking whom he may devour." If we are not vigilant, we may not see him coming until it is too late. Then he whispers his nasty lies in our ears, twisting and bending our minds, leaving us confused and incapable of making good choices. We practice daily vigilance to maintain daily victory and by continually seeking God's choices for us. This ensures us an abundant life in Christ.

Scripture Four: Job 12:10, 13, 16

> "In whose hand is the soul of every living thing, and the breath of all mankind. With Him is wisdom and strength, he hath counsel and understanding. With Him is strength and wisdom: the deceived and the deceiver are His."

God has taught us that through Christ Jesus we can do all things. He has also taught us how he imparts wisdom and strength to those who seek him, and now he is teaching us that he holds every living thing in his mighty hand, which includes Satan. This is how "the deceived and the deceiver are His."

God is the Alpha and the Omega, which means the beginning and the end. As the creator of all things, he created the angel Lucifer in heaven, and he was the most beautiful angel in all of heaven. Lucifer was very close to God, but his pride made him want to be God. Lucifer desired for every living thing God had created to worship him. Lucifer told God he could get as many people to worship him as worshiped God. After this declaration by Lucifer, God could not allow him to dwell in heaven with such an impure and prideful heart.

I can only imagine how disappointed God was when Lucifer fell from his grace. So God cast Lucifer into outer darkness, known as Hades or hell, to be eternally separated from God and his glory. Once Lucifer was cast out of heaven, his name was changed to Satan. Since God created all mankind and Satan, he alone holds "the soul of every living thing" in his hand, including "the deceived," meaning you and me, and "the deceiver," meaning Satan.

That is why our victory is found through Christ Jesus! Satan is compelled by his pride to seek whom he may devour in a futile effort to prove to God he can get as many people to worship him and be cast into hell as God can get to worship him and go to heaven. Thus, the root cause of spiritual warfare and why offenses must come. To maintain our spiritual victory, we must read and study the Scriptures. Hiding God's Holy Word in our heart helps us to stay vigilant, and understanding Satan's battle tactics helps us remain victorious.

Scripture Five: James 1:8 and Romans 8:13

> "A double minded man is unstable in all his ways."

> "For if ye live after the flesh, ye shall die: but if ye through the Spirit do mortify the deeds of the body, ye shall live."

If we are not vigilant and do not keep our minds on God, then we become unstable in our ways, meaning thoughts, actions, and reactions. This instability opens us up for Satan's attack. If we practice our vigilance daily, it will become second nature to us, and it will not be difficult to maintain our victory. However, we have to remember not to get too comfortable in our walk with Christ because that is when Satan will pounce. Our actions and reactions also let him know when we are unstable in our faith, which is what he is waiting for. When we become unstable in our faith, our Christian walk is crippled, and Satan will definitely be there to try to devour us. We must walk in the Spirit of the Lord because our continued victory lies with our vigilant focus on him and through the daily turning away from our fleshly sins.

Scripture Six: James 2:19 and Psalm 83:18

"Thou believest that there is one God; thou doest well: the devils also believe and tremble."

"That men may know that thou, whose name alone is *Jehovah*, art the most high over all the earth."

These scriptures confirm that we should believe in the one true God who governs "over all the earth," and his name is Jehovah. Even the devils "believe and tremble." Obviously, Satan's dominions chose to reject Jehovah and followed Satan all the way to their eternal hell. Recall Satan wanted to be God; therefore, his purpose is to seek those who are willing to reject Jehovah and follow him to hell. Beware of Satan because he is a false god and a master counterfeiter who can appear as an angel of light. God left his Holy Word to instruct, lead, guide, direct, and protect us from Satan. We maintain our victory over Satan by seeking understanding through the Bible. Therefore, we must be vigilant in going to Sunday school, church, and participating in Bible studies. It is very rewarding when God imparts his glorious wisdom allowing us, through the Scriptures, to understand more about our daily battles with Satan, his dominions, and spiritual warfare.

Scripture Seven: James 1:19

> "Wherefore, my beloved bretheren, let every man be swift to hear, slow to speak, slow to wrath: for the wrath of man worketh not righteousness of God."

This scripture from James is about wrath, which is another word for anger. In the previous chapter, "Good Grief," we learned how to give our anger to God. However, Satan uses our anger to manipulate or goad us into evil thoughts and bad reactions to the situation or confrontation at hand.

As brothers and sisters in Christ, we should be quick to hear spiritually and, with God's help, discern the truth from the lies. Once we discern the truth, we will see that Satan is the enemy behind the person he is manipulating. Then we will be able to speak the truth in love through the name of Jesus, casting Satan behind us. Our victory over Satan will resound through the heavens because we kept our anger under control and did not lose our spiritual walk through bad temperament. Therefore, we stay vigilant by seeking strength through Jesus Christ to peacefully resolve the issue or to walk away from the confrontation. In doing so, we stand victorious because Satan did not succeed in provoking us to anger or wrath.

The last line of the scripture reads, "The wrath of man worketh not righteousness of God," meaning God cannot reward us with righteousness if we allow Satan and his dominions to provoke us to misbehave in our Christian walk. When we allow Satan to provoke us, we are not living examples of God and his marvelous grace. Although it is difficult to turn and walk away from conflict, if we do not flee, we are no better than our transgressor. Think about it this way: if our behavior is not any different than his or hers, then we have lowered ourselves and allowed Satan to manipulate us too! It is hard to look at ourselves from this perspective, but we must if we are going to see how God sees us as he watches from heaven. God does not want us to get discouraged in our vigilance but rather be encouraged through our victory.

Scripture Eight: James 3:17

> "But the wisdom that is from above is first pure, then peaceable, gentle, and easy to be entreated, full of mercy and good fruits, without partiality, and without hypocrisy. And the fruit of righteousness is sown in peace of them that make peace."

What a beautiful verse. God is confirming that we should seek his wisdom because it is pure. Then we will be able to react with peaceful hearts and be gentle in our demeanor because we will have his understanding. Moreover, when we have God's understanding, our hearts will be like Jesus, and we will have mercy regardless of who Satan has put in front of us to tempt us to fail and lose our victory.

A vigilant attitude on our part will produce the fruit of righteousness, which can only be sown in the soil of one who has made peace in his or her heart with his or her enemy or transgressor. This is why we must forgive as soon as the transgression happens! Forgiveness allows us to keep our hearts fertile and filled with God's peace. Matthew 6:5 instructs us to pray and ask God to deliver us from evil and to forgive us as we forgave our trespasser. What better defense do we need to stand victorious over Satan?

Scripture Nine: James 4:3

> "Know this, that the trying of your faith worketh patience."

Trying times are designed to grow us spiritually and to teach us patience, provided we keep our hearts and minds on Jesus when we are going through them. Even though we are God's children, we will still have trials and tribulations to go through in our lives; however, we will be better equipped to handle them through Christ. Our heavenly Father knows what is best for us, and when we misbehave and fall into sin, it is his love that chastises us and brings us to a point of repentance.

If we find ourselves repeatedly going through the same trial, our question should not be, "Why me?" It should be, "Lord, what would you have me to learn from this?" Satan will deliberately set obstacles in our way to tempt us, hoping that we will stumble and eventually fall. Then the roaring lion will pounce upon us and try to devour us. His wickedness is endless, and he sets no boundaries. When we find ourselves in an endless cycle, repeating the same trials over and over, then we must seek God's will for our life and take the necessary steps to make the changes in our life that will be pleasing unto God.

Once we learn what God is ultimately trying to teach us, we will be able to recognize the cycles, turn from our ways, and put an end to them. When we do, God will reward us for our faithfulness. We will win the battle and claim our victory, but we must remain vigilant and not allow Satan to trip us up time and again.

Scripture Ten: 1 Timothy 2:26

> "And that they may recover themselves out of the snare of the devil, who are taken captive by him at his will."

Timothy is reminding us the devil tries to take us captive at his will, and he will be successful in keeping us in captivity unless we are vigilant. Because we are made of flesh, we may not always master our vigilance and may be snared by Satan on occasion. However, we can and will be recovered from the devil's snare through Christ. Even though we may find ourselves deceived and caught by Satan, it does not mean we have to dwell in his trap. We can reclaim our victory by calling on God. Through prayer, we should seek God's will in our lives. Hiding the Scriptures in our hearts and prayer are the two best battle tactics we have to conquer Satan. A vigilant prayer life keeps us focused on God or leads us back to him if we stumble, and God is the ultimate victor over Satan.

As children of God, we are heirs to the throne, and our inheritance makes us victorious also! What a marvelous thought to know we can conquer Satan through prayer as we gain our strength through Christ. We must be vigilant in our prayers and continue to seek victory through God's will for our lives.

Our victory song is Psalm 98:1: "O sing unto the Lord a new song; for He hath done marvelous things: His right hand and His holy arm, hath gotten Him the victory." We should always sing unto the Lord for the marvelous things he has done in our lives. When we call on his name, he sweeps us up into the safety of his holy arms. Cradled there, nothing can come against us that he cannot protect us from or help us through.

If we fail to seek God, we are separating ourselves from his protection. Once we separate ourselves from him and stop putting on our armor of God, we become open targets for Satan. Only when we are held in the cleft of God's wings do Satan's arrows of deception fall to the ground as God's glory deflects the wicked darts of lies and deceit. We see with spiritual eyes, hear with spiritual ears, and our hearts become more like Jesus. I used to think I could never live up to being a true Christian, but with the tools God has given us and continued vigilance, we can maintain our Christian walk and keep our victory over Satan. We are not perfect and can never be perfect this side of heaven. However, we can stand pure, holy, and blameless before the Lord, and that is certainly an attainable goal.

We have reached the end of victory lane, and through God's Scriptures we have learned how important it is to remain vigilant and maintain our victory over Satan. There is not a better time than now to begin applying the teachings of Jesus to your heart daily. Be vigilant by starting each day with prayer, put on the armor of God, submit your thoughts to the authority of Christ, and stand victorious over Satan every day. Sing your victory song!

The Joy of the Journey

My friend in healing, as you traversed your personal journey of courage, I sincerely pray God transformed your heart as you developed a personal relationship with him. This blessed journey was brought to you by Jesus Christ, who offered you God's ultimate healing. I pray you found peace in your spirit, love in your heart, stability in your mind, and comfort in your soul. I also pray your joy was restored and that you have renewed hope and stronger faith.

If you are still struggling with the aftermath of the sins committed against you, I urge you to look to the author and finisher of our faith and to find your joy in him. The Lord tells us in Scripture not to fear or be afraid. Fear will cause you to lose your joy. His Scripture also tells us not to worry about things we cannot change. Worrying is the product of a lack of faith. It has no value, it robs you of your joy, and it causes you to stumble in your walk. In addition, worry will break your spirit, and it accomplishes absolutely nothing. Granted, your circumstances may not always bring you joy, but regardless of your negative circumstances, you can find joy in the Lord if you only seek him, especially in the midst of the storms life blows your way. Do not allow Satan to bind you and rob you of the joy of your journey.

I hope you will continue to follow God and bask in the glory of his magnificent presence. If you do not attend church, please ask God to lead you to one. *Seek* his will in your life; then *listen* and *obey*. Never forget to put on your armor of God and give him control of your thoughts daily because Satan will never cease his attack against you. Always remember, if you asked God for forgiveness and turned from your sinful ways, then you are forgiven. Stay vigilant and maintain your victory through Jesus Christ!

I leave you now in the capable hands of God. Stay close to him through prayer and worship. Serve him in everything you do and continue the reconstruction of your heart daily. Be a sweet-smelling aroma unto the Lord and realize *the joy of the journey is the peace of God that surpasses all understanding.* May God's blessings be upon you as you live the rest of your life with the understanding that life is a continual *Journey of Courage.*

Until we meet in heaven, may the footsteps along your journey of life always lead to you to God, and may your joy always be found through Jesus Christ.

Bibliography

Holy Bible, King James Version, Thomas Nelson Incorporated, 1989.

Merriam-Webster's Collegiate Dictionary Tenth Edition, Merriam-Webster Incorporated 1996.

Dictionary.com_2009._11_June_2009_<http://www.dictionary.reference.com/browse/pride>.

Kubler-Ross, Elisabeth. *On Death and Dying,* Macmillan, NY 1969.